**KEEP THE
FAITH,
BABY!**

Also by Adam Clayton Powell

MARCHING BLACKS

KEEP THE FAITH, BABY!

BY ADAM CLAYTON POWELL

 TRIDENT PRESS NEW YORK 1967

Contents

**KEEP THE
FAITH,
BABY!**

"And All They
that Heard It
Wondered"

LUKE 2:18

And all they that heard it wondered at those things which
were told them by the shepherds.

Most of us feel that Christmas is the time to be childish, that it is an event for children.

However, to be childish is to be immature, and to refuse to face facts fairly and squarely. On the other hand, to be child-*like* is to have the spirit of a child.

This is one of the things that we of this present age need —to keep wonder in our life, for life without wonder is hardly worth living.

So at Christmas we celebrate the most wonderful event in the sweep of human history. It is wonderful by whatever standard we judge it. It is inconceivable that anyone can be so utterly devoid of imagination as to be untouched by the wonder of the birth of a new spirit in the world—the spirit of Christ.

Yet it is a fact that many, including a considerable number who call themselves Christians, have lost the wonder of Christmas. We will gape at Sputniks, gasp at gifts, and yet fail to feel the thrill of wonder when we realize what this Spirit has done and can do for our world.

Imagine for a moment the world in the course of human history without Jesus Christ.

The mind is sickened and the heart numbed at the thought of what might have been, what would have been inevitably the normal state of human affairs. Yes, it is true that today we live in a world with highly advanced techniques of destruction. But the Spirit of Christ at least casts some restraint on our current nightmare.

The celebration of Christmas could provide the only authentic emotion that could lift us out of this money-grabbing, war-weary and sin-sick world.

But the wonder of Christmas is not only dulled by easy familiarity but it is smothered by saccharine sentimentality and buried under the rubbish of commercialism.

Christmas today is identified with too many tricky, wishful-thinking greeting cards decorated with dear little kittens, sweet little puppy dogs, bells, balloons, candles, crackers, holly, mistletoe; but the real wonder of Christmas is that God Almighty became flesh and dwelt among men.

History records men such as Alfred *the Great,* William *the Conqueror,* Richard *the Lionhearted,* Edward *the Confessor,* Edward *the Peacemaker;* why can we not use the prophecy of Isaiah: "his name shall be called Wonderful . . ."

Jesus *the Wonderful* came as a deliverer. He delivers people from sin; from the guilt of sin; from the grief of sin; from the pain of sin; from the penalty of sin; from the power of sin. Jesus the Wonderful inaugurated a new age and a new social order.

If we will accept the meaning of the Christmas message, we will be able to create a society more wonderful than any utopian dreamer has ever thought of.

We have taken a world of trees and used them to become instruments upon which to hang the strange fruit of a human body.

We have taken the heavens, which were made to declare the glory of God, and used them as paths for missiles to carry H-bombs to destroy men made in the image of God.

We have taken the church of Jesus Christ and twisted it into the backbone of reaction and prejudice and segregation.

We have destroyed the wonder of Christianity and replaced it with the ordinariness of *church-anity*.

Things can happen in this world more wonderful than eye hath seen or ear hath heard or the heart of the most optimistic philosopher hath felt, if we would accept the Spirit of Christ.

He is wonderful because He does not come once a year to be discarded as a withered tree.

When the Spirit of Christ comes into our hearts, there comes an experience which reaches with its influence across the entire year.

He is wonderful because in Him there is no imperfection.

Contemplate the wonder of the life He lived: He lived well . . . labored well . . . bled well . . . loved well . . . laid down His life well. . . . He has done all things wonderfully well.

He is wonderful because He came to save a lost world.

Think with me now of humanity, all the billions who ever lived, of all classes, conditions, complexions, constitutions. Consider them as an immense avalanche moving steadily down the road to ruin!

No human energy could stop this avalanche, no human virtue could restrain it, no invention of man would have the power, no force would be available. Lost!

But Jesus is the wonderful one.

Only through Him was this tide of humanity made to turn.

All power is given unto me. (Matthew 28:18)

Black Power:
A Form of Godly Power

SONG OF SOLOMON 1:5–6

I am black, but comely, O ye daughters of Jerusalem . . .
Look not upon me, because I am black, because the sun
hath looked upon me . . .

PSALMS 62:11

God hath spoken once; twice have I heard this; that power
belongeth unto God.

ISAIAH 40:29–31

He giveth power to the faint; and to them that have no
might he increaseth strength.
Even the youths shall faint and be weary, and the young
men shall utterly fall:
But they that wait upon the Lord shall renew their
strength; they shall mount up with wings as eagles; they
shall run, and not be weary; and they shall walk, and not
faint.

In the last year and a half, a number of statements about "power" and, more recently, "black power" have been made by me.

Others have embraced the phrase "black power," more for their own misguided and selfish ends than in any sincere attempt to help the black masses.

Let me go back to March 28, 1965, when I spoke in Chicago and presented a "Black Position Paper for America's 20 million Negroes."

At that time I called for black people to seek "audacious power." Audacious power is the power that begins with the stand-up-and-be-counted racial pride in being black and thinking black. "I am black, but comely, O ye daughters of Jerusalem," said the peasant girl in the Song of Solomon.

On that same day, I outlined a seventeen-point plan for black people to build this "audacious power" within the Great Society. It was a kind of "Black Operation Bootstrap."

I urged black people to mobilize their political, economic, financial and educational power to build their communities into neighborhoods of excellence.

Then on May 29, 1966, in the baccalaureate at Howard University, I urged my people to pursue excellence and to purpose our lives to the fulfillment of divine-souled human rights instead of the narrow-souled civil rights.

I declared on that day: "To demand these God-given

human rights is to seek black power, audacious power—the power to build black institutions of splendid achievement."

Thus the phrase "black power" was born.

What is "black power"?

"Black power" has come to mean whatever any newspaper columnist, editorial writer, civil rights leader or white racist wants it to mean.

One of America's great statesmen, A. Philip Randolph, talks in terms of "coalition power."

Phrased another way, it is called by my beloved friend Rev. Martin Luther King, Jr., "striped power." (I called Martin the other day and told him that stripes are found on striped pants, which are worn by Baptist preachers and zebras. And nobody can ride a zebra.)

The National Urban League's Whitney Young conceptualized "black power" as the "green power" of the pocketbook. And indeed he should, because what organization has derived more green power from the civil rights movement than the National Urban League—the Wall Street of the civil rights movement? It can be rightfully said that the National Urban League has made a "killing" on the civil rights stock market with the more than $1 million it receives in grants from the federal government.

That fiery young radical Stokeley Carmichael sees "black power" as the fuse for rebellions in America's cities.

I cannot pretend to speak for what others interpret "black power" to mean.

I can only speak for Adam Clayton Powell. And in so doing, I only remind millions of black people of my thirty-six years of commitment to the cause of freedom for the black man.

First of all, black power is not anti-white.

Black power incorporates everybody who wishes to work together, vote together and worship together.

Is black power white supremacy in reverse?

Black power makes no moral judgment. But white supremacy does. Black power simply reaffirms the integrity, dignity and self-respect of black people. White supremacy denies them.

If white people can accept black leadership in any given political, business or educational situation—which is, in a sense, a kind of black power—then I, Adam Clayton Powell, welcome them, because, as Paul said: "There is neither Jew nor Greek, there is neither bond nor free, there is neither male nor female: for ye are all one in Christ Jesus." (Galatians 3:28)

But there are those who would run through the streets drunk with the "wine of violence," shouting "black power" in a purposeless scorched-earth orgy.

There are those who scream, "Burn, baby, burn," while pretending to be clothed in the majestic mantle of "black power."

Black power is a constructive approach to the new life of freedom for black people in the Great Society. Violence must play no part in its fulfillment.

Black power is the brain power that admonishes. Instead of "Burn, baby, burn," we should be shouting, "Learn, baby, learn" and "Earn, baby, earn."

Instead of lighting up the sky with Molotov cocktails, we should be brightening the skies with the stars of millions of registered voters in 1968.

Instead of throwing fire bombs, we should fire up our energies to build more black-owned businesses in our communities.

After years and years of rioting, black people should realize by now that when we burn up the neighborhood dry cleaners in a riot or a rebellion, we set our own clothes on fire.

When we loot our neighborhood stores, we steal the food from the mouths of black babies in our own communities.

When we destroy a store or business in the black com-

munity, we throw black people out of work. Is that what we
seek?

After the holocaust of last summer in Watts, only two
businesses returned to that charred community.

Where is the phoenix that should have risen out of the
ashes of Watts?

> Out of the heart's eternal torture fire
> No flaming Phoenix risen—
> Only the naked soul, spent with desire,
> Bursts its prison.
> —WILLIAM ROSE BENÉT, *Gaspara Stampa*, STANZA I

The black man's soul is trying to burst its prison of second-class citizenship, while the fires of segregation burn our
hopes for a better tomorrow.

Unfortunately, the explosions of America's so-called
race riots are not the only violence that stalks our streets today.

We are now agonizing through one of the most critical
breakdowns in law and order this nation has ever seen in its
history.

Isn't it ironic that it is perfectly safe for a man to take a
walk in space and return to his spaceship unharmed, but it is
unsafe for a man or a woman, black or white, to walk our streets
without being beaten.

Recently, here in Harlem, in the beloved Abyssinian
Baptist Church, a religious citadel for over forty-three years in
this community and 158 years in New York City, a young secretary was raped while working in the office.

Some time ago, in St. Peter's Roman Catholic Church in
Washington, D.C., only two blocks from the Capitol, a Congressional secretary was stabbed while kneeling at the altar in
prayer.

Sam Stafford, a prize-winning young white reporter, who
writes with compassion and understanding about the plight of

the poor, was jumped and beaten in Washington, D.C., by three hoodlums out for some fun.

Only two days ago, the stench of violence stained my office doors in Washington, D.C. A young black man who refused to leave my office after being unable to see me, attacked a Capitol Hill policeman and in the process was himself bloodied.

And why was he unable to see me?

Because I was meeting on the Senate-House Conference Report for the War on Poverty bill, a bill which is as much designed to help black people as any other piece of legislation coming out of the Congress.

All over this great land we are at war with ourselves. Is the sole cause of this new disorder in our society racial?

It is not! The young people of today—white and black— have lost respect for themselves, their parents, their teachers and their God.

In their impatience in this rocket age, which still uses rocking-chair methods to solve its human-relations problems, today's young people have refused to accept Plutarch's counsel:

> Perseverance is more prevailing than violence; and many things which cannot be overcome when they are together, yield themselves up when taken little by little.

Young people, black and white, are telling us: Give us the Great Society, or what I call the Guaranteed Society now, not "little by little" or by fits and starts.

It is not the older people who are asking, as *Time* magazine did on its cover, "Is God dead?" but our younger people, whose spiritual lives are vapid.

God is not dead. People are dead—dead to an awareness of God and his wondrous love for all mankind.

While I am worried about the increasing rate of crime in our streets and the breakdown in law and order in our communities among all citizens, I am still far more concerned about the inability of white America to save its democratic soul by learning to live with her black brothers and sisters.

Let me read a few sentences from a book. And as I read, ponder the significance of these words in the current mood of worsening race tensions in America:

> A pamphlet on "How to Prevent a Race Riot in Your Home Town" was issued in November 1943 by the American Civil Liberties Union through the Committee Against Racial Discrimination. The pamphlet was written by Winifred Raushenbush. During her investigation she found 23 cities where racial tensions are so acute that there is liable to be an explosion any day.
>
> This Negro minority not only hates the officers of the law but they hate anything that looks white. They would kill a white cat if one passed through their neighborhood.
>
> Behind all the immediate trouble, so far as the threat of overt action is concerned, is an impatient, irresistible drive of the Negroes on the one hand for a fuller realization of the equality which has long been promised to them, but just as long denied. On the other hand, stubborn, deepening and in some places broadening resistance of the whites to that very aim.

Were those words written last week, last month, or even three months ago?

They were not. They were written almost a quarter of a century ago—twenty-one years ago—by my father, Rev. A. Clayton Powell, Sr., in his book *Riots and Ruins*.

One Congressman, a member of my committee, happened to read a few parts of my father's book last week and remarked to me that it was as fresh in its meaning for today as if it were written last week.

My father harshly deplored the excesses of violence and the destructive goals of the scorched-earth policy in the freedom struggle. Yet he understood what drove the black man to these excesses.

"Don't ask who starts race riots which threaten to tear the Constitution of the United States and the Four Freedoms into fragments, thus nullifying everything that costs the world millions of lives and more than four hundred billion dollars," wrote my father in this same book.

He then discussed the race riots of his day—1943, 1944 and 1945—and almost prophetically wrote:

> Take your pencil and try to add up all the wrongs heaped upon the Negro for 326 years and you will get the answer to the ruinous avalanches that roared through Los Angeles, Beaumont, Mobile, Detroit and Harlem. . . . Walk down the street of any large city with a mixed racial population, talk with 50 men and women, and you will get at least a hundred different causes for riots. Casually analyze all of their reasons and you will find racial prejudice and hatred at the bottom of them.

What disturbs me most about those words which I have quoted from my father's book written twenty-one years ago is that it could have been written today! My father is talking about conditions which still exist today—1966!

He does not use the terms "black power" and "white backlash," but these concepts are implicit in his thinking.

Oh, yes, median family incomes of black middle-class people have risen, more Negroes can play on golf courses today than they did in 1945, swimming pools are open and more Negroes have Cadillacs and split-level houses. We even have Negroes living in suburbia.

But how do you define progress when black people pillage and burn their own homes and businesses in Watts, hysterically screaming, "Get Whitey!"?

What has happened to progress when a mob of white adults attack little black children with clubs and chains in Grenada, Mississippi, simply because those little black children are trying to go to school?

We have indulged ourselves in the past five years in a magnificent exercise of near futility with our marches, our sit-ins, our demonstrations, our picketing and now our rebellions.

True, we have shocked the white man to a shivering perception of the black man's chained despair.

But we can count no conversions.

We have transformed few minds. We have made no radical changes in the economic servitude of the black masses.

This is why black people can no longer continue to rely solely on white people or new civil rights laws to bail them out of the jail of second-class citizenship.

Black people themselves must exercise a massive responsibility for their fate. Black people themselves must assume control and direction of their destiny.

How? I say "black power" is the path we must tread.

If whites will only listen for a moment, they will realize there is no hate, no violence nor anti-white feelings in the "black power" I seek for black people.

Black power is, *first and foremost,* Godly power. "God hath spoken once; twice have I heard this; that power belongeth unto God." (Psalms 62:11) "For God hath not given us the spirit of fear; but of power . . ." (II Timothy 1:7)

Without the hand of God in man's hand, there can be no coming together of black and white in this world. The deterioration of white power is its failure to incorporate God in its way of life.

Unless man is committed to the belief that all of mankind are his brothers, then he labors in vain and hypocritically in the vineyards of equality.

Second, black power is black pride—"I am black, but comely, O ye daughters of Jerusalem."

It is this pride, this belief in self and in the dignity of the black man's soul that Senegal President Leopold Senghor emphasizes when he speaks of *"la negritude."*

To Senghor *"la negritude"* is the cry of an in-gathering for all black people to be proud of their black culture, their black roots. This is where "black power" also begins.

Third, black power is black initiative—the arousing of black people from fear and the sad fatigue of idleness to take the initiative by lifting themselves up and changing their lives through the mobilization of the energies of millions of black people in black communities all over America.

Fourth, black power is black productivity—the increase of black jobs for black men and women, the contribution of black people to the gross national product, the beautification of black neighborhoods, and the expansion of black businesses.

In the ashen wake of San Francisco's recent riots, Mayor Shelley made history by his honest assessment of the underlying causes of those riots. The mayor implored President Johnson by telegram, "in the name of God and all human decency," to provide federal funds for jobs in his city.

Those riots, as have so many of the riots in our big cities, confronted us all with the ugly reality of one inescapable fact: while unemployment for whites has continued to decline, unemployment for black people has risen in the last twelve months.

A man's respect for law and order exists in precise relationship to the size of his paycheck. Find jobs for the black jobless in our cities and the cooling breezes of employment will lower the hot temperatures in our streets.

Fifth, black power is black responsibility—the recognition by black people that they must demand and have a proportionate share of the responsibilities of running the communities, the cities and the states in which they live.

This responsibility is more than more black Congressmen, black mayors, or more city councilmen and state assemblymen. It is individual responsibility—an active involvement by each individual in the political, educational, religious and economic life of his community.

In this era of black power—a peaceful and constructive approach to the problems of black people—and the so-called white backlash—a fear-ridden and destructive reaction to these problems—I am hopeful that America can rediscover its democratic soul to forge a new togetherness among all its citizens.

Whites must join hands with blacks to achieve the full freedom of the Guaranteed Society because they are determined to get their full measure of freedom.

As I wrote twenty-two years ago in my book *Marching Blacks:*

> The black man continues on his way. He plods wearily no longer—he is striding freedom road with the knowledge that if he hasn't got the world in a jug, at least he has the stopper in his hand. He wants to do the best that the world denied him. He is ready to throw himself into the struggle to make the dream of America become flesh and blood, bread and butter, freedom and equality. . . . He does not want the day of victory to be obtained through violence and bloodshed. But of one thing he is positive. In the words of Sherwood Eddy, writing in his *Pilgrimage of Ideas*—"In the wrong way or in the right way, through violence or nonviolence, it will surely come."

I, Adam Clayton Powell, hope that day of victory comes through nonviolence, but the choice is up to America to make—a choice that will fulfill God's prophecy to both Matthew and Isaiah:

And, behold, one of them which were with Jesus stretched out his hand, and drew his sword, and struck a servant of the high priest's, and smote off his ear.

Then said Jesus unto him, Put up again thy sword into his place: for all they that take the sword shall perish with the sword. (Matthew 26:51–52)

Violence shall no more be heard in thy land, wasting nor destruction within thy borders; but thou shalt call thy walls Salvation, and thy gates Praise. . . .

A little one shall become a thousand, and a small one a strong nation: I the Lord will hasten it in his time. (Isaiah 60:18, 22)

A Living Book for a Dying World

EZEKIEL 33:1–7

Again the word of the Lord came unto me, saying,

Son of man, speak to the children of thy people, and say unto them, When I bring the sword upon a land, if the people of the land take a man of their coasts, and set him for their watchman:

If when he seeth the sword come upon the land, he blow the trumpet, and warn the people;

Then whosoever heareth the sound of the trumpet, and taketh not warning; if the sword come, and take him away, his blood shall be upon his own head. . . .

But if the watchman see the sword come, and blow not the trumpet, and the people be not warned; if the sword come, and take any person from among them, he is taken away in his iniquity; but his blood will I require at the watchman's hand.

So thou, O son of man, I have set thee a watchman unto the house of Israel; therefore thou shalt hear the word at my mouth, and warn them from me.

We are living in a dying world. We have already fought a thirty-five-year war and today it looks as if it is going to be a fifty-year war. We live in a century of starvation in the midst of plenty; of concentration camps in the midst of unparalleled education; of unexampled brute terror in a world of enlightenment. We have darkness: instead of peace there is violence; instead of freedom there is the rise of authority; instead of security there is the mood of anxiety. We might as well tighten our emotional belts and settle down to the prospects of living all of our days in the midst of strain. "Peace in our time" is a great dream but we shall not live to see it.

Some of us thought that we were going to live in a world in which progress was inevitable. Our optimism was childish. Today, long after the terror of Nazism and Fascism, we still witness Protestants in Spain being arrested for publishing their teachings or distributing the word of God.

Never were promises so grand and failure so apparent. We have been oversold on what science could do for mankind. We are face to face with bitterness in air-conditioned penthouses, and gross injustice among people driving streamlined cars. Toynbee points out that increasing command over our environment only makes a society which is in disintegration have greater driving power for its chosen work of self-destruction.

Whatever our age may be, we surely are not optimistic and cannot be.

Our world is decaying and dying.

A saint like Schweitzer draws fewer people than a basket-ball game.

In our national life we worship mediocrity and our leadership constantly reflects this.

The American Fascists who propagated Hitlerism during World War II are now in the saddle and are smearing with their cry of "Communist" all those who led the fight to unite with the Soviet to defeat Hitler, even though they are standing with democracy against world Communism.

No one dares to stand in a public-place to point the finger of truth at them—we have lost our moral nerve!

For the first time in the history of the world the entire population is in peril at every single point on the surface of our earth.

Yet I must come today to say that we can "sing the Lord's song in a strange land."

The very words of this Living Book came out of times of the greatest calamity.

We can, therefore, make this time of strain a time of greatness.

I preach today to you the sentinels of Israel, the watchmen of God, and I take as my text the prophecy of Ezekiel in Chapter 33.

Who are we?

We are God's watchmen. We are all that is left. We are the remnant. We are the bridge across which humanity must walk from out of this dying world of darkness into a new world of light.

But as Ezekiel pointed out, there are good and there are bad watchmen. The distinguishing mark is whether we do or do not blow the trumpet and sound the warning.

What must we blow the trumpet against? We must blow the trumpet against:

Materialism and the profit motive;

Secularism and encroachment in the church;

Totalitarianism and the world state of any ism;

Racism and universal military training on a Dixie pattern.

Sound the warning—through this Living Book!

The first warning is against Materialism: "Thou shalt have no other gods before me." (Exodus 20:3) "Before the mountains were brought forth . . . even from everlasting to everlasting, thou *art* God." (Psalms 90:2)

The second warning is against Secularism: "One lord, one faith, one baptism." (Ephesians 4:5) There is only one way: "I am the way, the truth and the life." (John 14:6)

The third warning is against Totalitarianism: "This is my Father's world."

The fourth warning is against Racism—"Behold, how good and how pleasant it is for brethren to dwell together in unity." (Psalms 133:1)

The personal responsibility of each of us is inescapable: "his blood will I require at the watchman's hand."

We are not saved through any goodness of our own.

All of our righteousness is but filthy rags.

This is the key: We are sentinels to warn the people not to be Pharisees, not to think they are better than others.

"O son of man, I have set thee a watchman unto the house of Israel . . ."

God has brought us to such an hour as this. He has not led us as sheep before their shearers. He has not brought us into this decaying world to be slaughtered; we come equipped. He has placed the word of God—a Living Book—in our hand; a "sword of truth" if you please. In fact, it is "sharper than any two-edged sword."

I stand here today, a modern preacher, a so-called radi-

cal, and charge you to stand on the watch. In the midst of this
dying world, let the Living Book give you the strength to "blow
the trumpet" and "sound the alarm." Hide God's Word in your
heart; it will warm you.

> Let it be a lamp unto your feet.
> Let it light your pathway.
> Study it with your mind.
> The Living Book will quicken your spirit.
> The Word will strengthen thee and sustain thee.
> It will make a way out of no way.
> It will be a light that shines in darkness.

> If . . . my words abide in you, ye shall ask what ye will,
> and it shall be done unto you. (John 15:7)

The cry is beginning to go up from all over the earth:
"Watchman, what of the night?" (Isaiah 21:11) What is our
answer? "The night is far spent, the day is at hand: let us therefore cast off the works of darkness, and let us put on the armour
of light." (Romans 13:12)

I stand as a fellow sentinel of God in the midst of a
dying world. I see "not . . . peace, but a sword," (Matthew
10:34) "nation [rising] against nation" (Matthew 24:7) and
the "love of many [waxing] cold," (Matthew 24:12) but I
stand here to assure you that the dawn is coming. In the language of Henry Thoreau, ". . . only that day dawns to which
we are awake. There is more day to dawn. The sun is but a
morning star."

I see the dawn coming. It is coming through: awakened
Protestantism; alerted ministry; a fellowship pew; a witnessing
church, and a saving Gospel.

Let us heed the words of William Pierson Merrill:

> Rise up, O men of God!
>   Have done with lesser things,

Give heart, and soul, and mind, and strength
   to serve the King of Kings.
Rise up, O men of God!
   His Kingdom tarries long.
Bring in the day of brotherhood
   And end the night of wrong.
Lift high the cross of Christ!
   Tread where His feet have trod:
As brothers of the Son of Man,
   Rise up, O men of God!

Harlem

JOSHUA 1:1–9

Now after the death of Moses the servant of the Lord it came to pass, that the Lord spake unto Joshua the son of Nun, Moses' minister, saying,

Moses my servant is dead; now therefore arise, go over this Jordan, thou, and all this people, unto the land which I do give to them, even to the children of Israel.

Every place that the sole of your foot shall tread upon, that have I given unto you, as I said unto Moses.

From the wilderness and this Lebanon even unto the great river, the river Euphrates, all the land of the Hittites, and unto the great sea toward the going down of the sun, shall be your coast.

There shall not any man be able to stand before thee all the days of thy life: as I was with Moses, so I will be with thee: I will not fail thee, nor forsake thee. . . .

Have not I commanded thee? Be strong and of a good courage; be not afraid, neither be thou dismayed: for the Lord thy God is with thee whithersoever thou goest.

What is Harlem?

A stretch of real estate running from 110th Street to 155th Street and the East River to the Hudson River? Or is it a ghetto of segregation? A crime-racked, welfare-aid-saturated concentration camp of slum housing, dope peddling and gambling? Or is it a community of churches? Or simply the world-renowned capital of Negro America?

Harlem is all of those things and more. Whatever it is or is not, Harlem is at the bottom a frame of mind, a way of thinking, a way of looking at the world.

With 431,330 people, it is bigger than all of Newark, New Jersey, and just slightly smaller than Phoenix, Arizona. In size Harlem would rank as the thirtieth largest city in America.

Of New York State's forty-one Congressional districts, the Eighteenth Congressional District, which is essentially Harlem, has the lowest median family income—$3,993 per year.

That's only $993 above the poverty level.

Crime is up in New York City 21 percent over last year, and over half of all the narcotics addicts in America live in Harlem.

Negroes constitute over 70 percent of welfare recipients of the city's half-billion dollars spent on welfare yearly. Negroes are not lazy or welfare-prone—they just can't find jobs. And racial discrimination helps perpetuate unbroken progressions of welfare beggars.

Despite new housing projects, the city is losing its assault on slum housing in Harlem. Of Harlem's 150,339 housing units, fully one-third (52,044) were classified as deteriorating; 14,817 units were classified as dilapidated.

But Harlem's economic problems can be traced directly to racial discrimination in employment, which has produced chronic unemployment. Over half the people in Harlem (51 percent) work in jobs classified in the menial and unskilled categories or the lowest salary level. Just how serious is the problem of racial discrimination in all of New York City is revealed by U.S. Census figures, which show that 63 percent of all Negro wage earners in New York City are in the menial and unskilled categories.

Although Harlem's Negro population constitutes over 20 percent of the voters in this city, Negroes hold only 6 percent of the judgeships and 6 percent of the top jobs in City Hall. Negroes are the quintessence of the Democratic Party's political strength in New York City and, by logical extension, New York State.

Yet with this numerical strength, with all this political power, we still are unable to call our political souls our own and we recently witnessed the spectacle of Mayor Wagner of this city running roughshod over the combined wishes and preferences of the Harlem Assembly District leaders acting in concert to choose the Manhattan Borough President.

It is not that we sought to name the Manhattan Borough President, but only to suggest several possibilities. The Mayor's callous snub was directed to the district leaders but insulted 431,330 black people.

De facto segregation in Harlem's schools continues to plague this community's intellectual development, and this is an unchallengeable fact: Harlem's schools are still inferior educationally to the educational norm of this city.

As rich as is the culture of the black man in America,

there is no center that proudly showcases the Negro's cultural enrichment of America.

The Schoenberg Library is a small start, but there is no great center where works of art and sculpture, literary achievements, music (we invented, developed and now *own* jazz all by ourselves) could be displayed, where a legitimate theater could be developed. Such a center should also exhibit the achievements of Negroes in politics, public office, science, education and religion. We have given much to this land.

It is time for the Negroes of Harlem to rise up and claim their land.

> Moses my servant is dead; now therefore arise, go over this Jordan, thou, and all this people, unto the land which I do give to them, even to the children of Israel.
>
> Every place that the sole of your foot shall tread upon, that have I given unto you, as I said unto Moses. . . .
>
> There shall not any man be able to stand before thee all the days of thy life: as I was with Moses, so I will be with thee: I will not fail thee, nor forsake thee.

What are the requirements for Harlem? They are three: courage, strength and perseverance.

> Be strong and of a good courage: for unto this people shalt thou divide for an inheritance the land, which I sware unto their fathers to give them.

On Perseverance:

> Only be thou strong and very courageous, that thou mayest observe to do according to all the law, which Moses my servant commanded thee: turn not from it to the right hand or to the left, that thou mayest prosper withersoever thou goest.

This is God's Word.

This book of the law shall not depart out of thy mouth; but thou shalt meditate therein day and night, that thou mayest observe to do according to all that is written therein; for then thou shalt make thy way prosperous, and then thou shalt have good success.

God has promised Harlem he will build a new land for us if we but follow him.

Have not I commanded thee? Be strong and of a good courage; be not afraid, neither be thou dismayed: for the Lord thy God is with thee whithersoever thou goest.

Harlem stands at the crossroads of history today and as the country moves forward into the "Great Society," which way will and can Harlem move?

Can Harlem mobilize its human resources into a creative partnership with federal, state and municipal forces to become the symbol of progress for black people all over the world?

Can Harlem's citizens in this great twentieth century— the most productive and exciting period in mankind's history— uplift themselves and get up off their knees and walk straight as men and women, no longer children?

Can Harlem's folks, in a strong, unyielding bond with its churches and its ministers, lead the way for the rest of New York City in providing the moral climate that will rid this city of crime and corruption?

It can and it shall. Negroes can claim Harlem as their own and make it their land by placing their trust in God.

Pass through the host, and command the people, saying, Prepare you victuals; for within three days ye shall pass over this Jordan, to go in to possess the land, which the Lord your God giveth you to possess it.

—JOSHUA 1:11

Minimum Living—
Minimum Religion

LUKE 6:38

Give, and it shall be given unto you; good measure, pressed down, and shaken together, and running over, shall men give into your bosom. For with the same measure that ye mete withal it shall be measured to you again.

This world has lost its sense of discipline. The old authority has vanished and just at the very moment in history when discipline and authority are needed most, the emancipation of women, the freedom of black Africa and brown Asia and the islands of the seas, increased education for the masses, easy dissemination of information through press, radio and television and Telstar—all these have given man a new sense of freedom but without the authority and discipline to direct that freedom into constructive channels.

Man will not tolerate dictators, dogmas or dictatorial religion.

Man will not listen to man just because of his position.

Therefore, I present to you the only discipline and authority that can unite this wonderful world into a world of progress: a religion of authority.

Jesus faced the dictators of His day. He faced dictatorial religion, and yet the Scripture records that He taught as one having authority, not as the scribes.

He never held an office in the church.

He was never a priest, or rabbi, or bishop, or pastor.

He had an inner authority.

Only when we have an inner authority can we live to the maximum—maximum living, maximum faith and maximum religion.

"Give, and it shall be given unto you; good measure,

pressed down, and shaken together, and running over, shall men give into your bosom. For with the same measure that ye mete withal it shall be measured to you again."

Regardless of how full our material and intellectual lives may be, until we have the inner authority we will live fragmented—fragmentary thinking, fragmentary living and fragmentary preaching, which leads to minimum faith.

Minimum faith is one that stays on the surface, where even the ritual of the church has no power and brings no joy.

But maximum faith is one that goes from death unto life, that allows one to live vitally in the midst of scorn and the storm of public opinion.

Maximum faith is not something that we have to carry, but something that carries us.

When we have a maximum religion, then we have the authority of religious certainty and religious conviction. This authority is born of the conviction that we are co-workers with God, working at the heart of the universe, and that there is an eternal goodness.

If you carry God in your heart, God will carry you in His hands.

Mix a conviction with a man and something happens!

You find maximum living and are transformed—ahead of the times; the shadow of the yet-to-be; critical of the status quo; exposing with burning words the inconsistencies, injustices and inadequacies of minimum living, of modern society; ever demanding reforms; refusing to be part of the establishment and the system.

This can only be done by men inspired by something greater than themselves. "His mother saith unto the servants, Whatsoever he saith unto you, do it." (John 2:5)

Then, and only then, with maximum faith and maximum religion and maximum living, can we raise up a generation of prophets who can stand in the gloom and darkness of our day, in the midst of the cheap values and the calculated hypocrisy, and cry: "He is not here; He is risen."

He is not here, bound by man-discovered laws.

He is not here, chained by man-created customs.

He is not here, buried by man-invented prejudices.

No, the spirit of Christ is risen—

Risen above our weaknesses.

Risen above our guilt.

Risen above our failures.

Risen above our sins.

And the angel answered and said unto the women, Fear not ye: for I know that ye seek Jesus, which was crucified.

He is not here: for he is risen, as he said. Come, see the place where the Lord lay.

And go quickly, and tell his disciples that he is risen from the dead; and, behold, he goeth before you into Galilee; there shall ye see him: lo, I have told you. (Matthew 28:5–7)

Regardless of how bad life is or seems to be, He goeth before you.

"Yea, though I walk through the valley of the shadow of death, I will fear no evil: for thou *art* with me . . ." (Psalms 23:4)

When the failures of life take you to hell, He goeth before you.

When the victories of life lift you to heaven, He goeth before you.

When the problems of minimum living, of friends and acquaintances, scatter you to the outermost parts of the earth, even there, He goeth before you.

There is no moment of loneliness.

No hour of sorrow.

No day of tragedy.

No night of fear.
No week of hopelessness.
No month of defeat.
No year of failure.
But only an eternity of salvation!

The
Imperishable Dream

JANUARY 7, 1962

GENESIS 37:19–20

And they said one to another, Behold, this dreamer cometh.

Come now therefore, and let us slay him, and cast him into some pit, and we will say, Some evil beast hath devoured him: and we shall see what will become of his dreams.

For some people the past year was the most undistinguished of their lifetime.

Not a single new idea was put forward.

Not a single great truth was spoken.

Not a single blow for freedom was struck.

Not a single invention or discovery was made.

All this is due to the fact that most of us have increasingly been growing accustomed to the philosophy of "getting by" —getting by with the least amount of effort and the least amount of energy. This is what I call the philosophy of the minimum.

But today I want to talk about "This year can be a better year." Of course, to most of you today this seems to be dreaming. But I want to point out that there is no disgrace in dreaming. In fact, dreams are extremely valuable.

But they are valuable only to the degree that they incite you to make them realities.

However, when dreams do not incite you to make them reality, you endanger your very life. And so you have your choice if you are a dreamer: a choice between a future and your life.

I would like to bring before you this morning two beautiful verses from the thirty-seventh chapter of Genesis:

> Behold, this dreamer cometh . . . let us slay him . . . and we shall see what will become of his dreams.

Dreamers have never been popular figures.

To attempt to see beyond the immediate present and to envision a better future usually makes one the object of ridicule, and sometimes even persecution.

Yet every forward step that the human race has taken has been the result of some great dreamer.

All progress today, material and spiritual, has come about because somebody dreamed a dream.

America lay undiscovered until one day a great dreamer dreamed of finding the western shore of the Atlantic Ocean. He had the courage, the daring, the faith to put his dream into execution, and he discovered the Americas.

Woodrow Wilson dared to dream the dream of a world union of nations. He dared to dream the dream that the time would come when war would cease forever. He tried to interpret to selfish generations of Americans his dream of a League of Nations. We laughed him out of the court of world opinion. We dismissed his dream as the impractical theory of an impossible idealist. We called him a starry-eyed dreamer.

And we paid for this with World War II.

The dreamer I am talking about today was named Joseph, a most beloved and popular character of the Old Testament.

I like to think of him as the most Christlike character that lived before Jesus came. The scene opens on the plains of Dothan. Jacob had sent his sons with the flocks and herds, seeking pasture land. After a few days he sent his next to youngest son, Joseph, who was the favorite of all his twelve sons, to find out how things were going with his brothers. But because Joseph was the favorite and because he was a dreamer, his brothers envied him.

Uncontrolled envy always leads to hatred.

And so they hated him. And as they looked across the plains of Dothan and saw him coming, they conspired against him, and said one to another, "Behold, this dreamer cometh; let's kill him and see what becomes of his dreams."

Only due to the wise counsel of the oldest brother, Reuben, did they decide not to kill him. Instead, they sold him to a caravan of Midianites who were passing by at that time on their way to Egypt. They stripped him of his beautiful coat of many colors that his old father, Jacob, had given to him. They dipped it in the blood of a goat and took it back to Jacob and said, "We found this coat in the thicket." And Jacob, the old man, cried in anguish, "My son has been devoured by some wild beast."

When Joseph arrived in Egypt, Potiphar, in charge of Pharaoh's royal guard, bought him. And then things began to happen to this dreamer who had been sold into slavery, whose brothers thought they had killed his dream.

In the first place, Potiphar realized that his home had become blessed because of the slave boy's presence. He loved him devotedly and trusted him with everything that he had on earth.

And then Potiphar's wife fell in love with him and she tried to do everything that she could to win him. But Joseph said, "How can I sin against God?" So rather than betray this woman, who made false accusations against him, he accepted the punishment of Potiphar and was thrown into prison.

He hadn't been in prison long when Pharaoh himself had him released so that Joseph could tell him about the dreams that were worrying him. Joseph interpreted the dreams as God's warning that there would be seven years of plenty and then seven years of famine.

The great king was so impressed that he ordered Joseph's immediate release and appointed him the head of the O.P.A. of Egypt.

Sure enough, the seven years of famine followed the seven years of plenty. And the Egyptians, because of Joseph's closeness to God, were able to weather the storm.

When the famine reached the household of old Jacob, and they heard that down in Egypt there was grain aplenty, the old man sent his sons down to Egypt to buy grain, that they might not die of starvation.

When they arrived they did not recognize their brother Joseph.

They were ushered into the presence of the most powerful man of all Egypt. Joseph recognized them. Finally, after many tests, he stood before them and said, "I am Joseph your brother, whom ye sold into Egypt."

They were terror-stricken, but Joseph, exercising the forgiveness that would make Christ famous one day said, "I am your brother whom you sought to destroy. Draw near, receive my forgiveness, my blessings, my gifts. Bring my father and the entire family, and all of you come and live in Egypt."

The story ends with Joseph, now an old man, dreaming his last dream on earth, calling his children and grandchildren about him, saying, "One day after I am dead there will arise a pharaoh who will not know me, Joseph, nor my people. You will become slaves, but nevertheless, one of these days, in God's good time, He will deliver our people and will lead them back to Canaan. When I die, embalm my body, place it in a coffin, but do not bury it in Egypt. Take my body back to Canaan when you go."

Four hundred years passed away, and the great Exodus began under the leadership of Moses. Way up at the head of the procession was a casket bearing the body of the great dreamer of the ages.

This year can be a better year.

A dream? Yes! But it is a dream that must be in intimate harmony with all the plans of God.

Nothing can be better, no one can be better, unless there is a direct relation between your plan and God's plan.

Joseph refused to yield to the moral standards of Egypt. He insisted on following the standards of Canaan, of God. And as a result Joseph went to prison rather than change his way of life, change his dreams.

This year can be a better year if you will stay close to God through prayer.

I do not, for a moment, believe that God warns us of everything to come, but I do know that if we stay close to Him we will be prepared for whatever does come. That's how Joseph was able to tell Pharaoh of the seven years of plenty and the seven years of famine.

This year can be a better year if we will stop consuming ourselves with revenge, and envy, and hatred. Joseph had every reason to hate his brothers, to get even with them. But he did not.

He knew that it is not within the province of man to judge man. He knew that there was one great Lord. ". . . be sure your sin will find you out." (Numbers 32:23) "Be not deceived; God is not mocked: for whatsoever a man soweth, that shall he also reap." (Galatians 6:7)

How much better it would be for us ourselves, our personalities, our friends, our environment, if we would only stop judging each other and start forgiving! That's what Joseph did. He said, "Draw near, receive my blessing, my forgiveness, my gifts."

Forgive your trespassers. Make this year a better year by renewing your faith in God, and your dreams will live forever.

What We Must Do about Africa

APRIL 3, 1960

ISAIAH 58:6

Is not this the fast that I have chosen? to loose the bands of wickedness, to undo the heavy burdens, and to let the oppressed go free, and that ye break every yoke?

Today the dark continent of Africa moves with rapidity toward its goal of freedom.

Last week's tragedy in South Africa, when the police shot more than 250 African political demonstrators, at least seventy-two of them fatally, by official count, has drawn racial tensions to a critical point. Maybe not South Africa but the rest of the entire civilized world is still in a state of shock over this grim affair.

Such acts of tyranny and despotism against a helpless people could well serve as the perfection of a triggering mechanism which could be fatal to these self-appointed masters.

An economic boycott would strangle the South African government into changing its course, which is now sad and hopeless, into one where liberty and equality for black as well as white would prevail.

There is a growing realization among South Africans that their country is out of step in its racial policies, not only with the rest of sub-Sahara Africa, but with the rest of the world. The feeling received considerable stimulus from a speech last month in Capetown, when British Prime Minister Macmillan warned that a "wind of change" was blowing throughout the continent.

Nevertheless, the Nationalist Party government, headed by Prime Minister Hendrik F. Verwoerd, has thus far shown little disposition to make any basic change in its policy of white supremacy and continued segregation, other than a stepped-up program of maiming and killing African natives.

The root of the problem is in numbers. There are 3 million whites and about 11.5 million persons whose skins are black or brown. Nearly 10 million of these are Africans. The whites, dreading that they will be overwhelmed, are afraid to grant the African full political rights and freedom.

Let us dwell for a moment on the speech of Prime Minister Macmillan. Certainly it was drafted in London more than two months before it was delivered. There has probably never been so polished, so adroit a speech made in that South African parliamentary dining room, or in any other chamber of the parliament.

It was a fit and proper occasion for the British Prime Minister, the first to visit South Africa while in office. History was in the making. He looked lonely on the dais, rather like a prisoner, standing between the Speaker and the President on one side, the Prime Minister of the Union and the leader of the opposition on the other.

Gazing out, he could look upon a painting portraying the whole National Convention of 1909. Suddenly, they seemed to have turned in their seats to listen to him.

The speech was not heavily applauded by his audience except when Mr. Macmillan said he deplored the "boycott." But Macmillan was speaking to a much larger, unseen audience, even though not one black representative was among the 230 listeners. His words, curiously hesitant and yet flowing, were far more disturbing.

Never before in the history of South Africa had the lords and leaders of white supremacy been spoken to so straightforwardly.

The recent riots in South Africa can in no way be described as reactions against the government's apartheid policy only.

These disturbances are the result of the present-day fight for freedom by the enslaved people of Africa.

Dr. Verwoerd and his government have attempted to place the mass murders of unarmed Africans by white soldiers and the gendarmerie in perspective. His views and the views of his butcher, Minister of Justice François Christian Erasmus, are brutally simple in that, according to their theory, mass repression must be regarded as the normal pattern of life in South Africa for the blacks!

Human thought, like God, makes the world in its own image. It transforms the social world into a better understanding of its fellow beings.

The renaissance, or new birth, for the native South African is in essence a sublime and impassioned spirituality. It has a divine and universal ideal. This is the reason why its passions have spread beyond its borders and received acclaim.

Therefore, those who limit it mutilate the superiority of moral sovereignties—the sovereignty of right over force; intelligence over prejudice; people over government; equality and reasoning over forced authority. They mutilate the revolution of ideas and ideals, the gospel of social rights and the broad charter of humanity.

History is filled with epochs of the human race during which decayed branches fall from the tree of humanity; when governments and their order of things grow old and outmoded. It is then that they fail to leave space for fresh ideas from their successors, which could lift the country to a much higher plane than before, thus recasting a more solid foundation for its people.

Therefore let us take account and lend our strength to these unarmed hordes, who are daily sacrificing their blood in their forward march to freedom, equality and democracy.

I propose that the following measures be undertaken:

First, that we ask for the immediate resignation of the Honorable Douglas Dillon, present Undersecretary of State, appointed June 12, 1959; formerly Undersecretary of Economic Affairs of the United States Government, appointed June 30, 1958.

Mr. Dillon was Chairman of the Dillon-Read Corporation. This corporation floated all bond issues for the Union of South Africa, and on December 2, 1958, was instrumental in raising a loan of $25 million. This seems to us a conflict of interest.

I do not see how it is possible to protest in the United Nations Security Council, while the number-two man of the Department of State has been involved in affairs with the bloody Boers in the Union of South Africa.

Second, we should call for a boycott of the Union of South Africa's diamonds. In 1957 the total sales were $48 million; the duties on this paid to the government of the Union of South Africa were $5 million, and the diamond profits tax was $6 million. The governments of Guiana, Ghana and Sierra Leone—black and free—produced more diamonds than the Union of South Africa. We should therefore shift our purchases from South Africa to West Africa.

Third, one of the largest businesses is the importation of African lobster tails. From this meeting today should go a resolution urging the AFL-CIO, and the longshoremen in particular, to refuse to unload any shipments of South African lobster tails and, instead, let us import our lobsters from the Bahamas.

Fourth, according to information furnished me by the Economics Division of the Library of Congress, the statistical abstract of the United States and the foreign grants statistics of the United States Department of Commerce, we the United States of America, while raising our voices in protest, have nevertheless loaned in credits to the Union of South Africa the following: 1952—$26 million; 1953—$35 million; 1954—$31 million; 1955—$21 million. From the first of July, 1945, to the thirtieth of September, 1959, gross credit was $148 million. This was used mainly for military equipment only. Owed to the Export-Import Bank is $92 million.

This, I demand, should be stopped immediately.

Fifth, we should demand that the International Bank for Reconstruction and Development cease its hypocrisy. As late as 1956, in answer to my protest, they said that they had loaned the Union of South Africa, $75 million to expand its railroad service and $60 million to increase the supply of electricity. As a result of a sharp protest by me, the International Bank wrote me that "benefits would be expected to accrue to the colored and native populations of the Union of South Africa as a result of projects financed with the help of the World Bank."

Finally, we should lay plans to picket the Union of South Africa's headquarters here in New York, and should make a study of what members of Congress are in favor of backing up our Congressional program.

The Africa we must help to create, the Africa we must bequeath to posterity, the Africa of our dreams, must be an Africa that is *free* from foreign domination.

It must be an Africa that the world will look toward and say, "Here is a continent of human beings who live up to the ideals of human society."

It must be an Africa which can fulfill John Donne's prophecy that: "No man is an island entire of itself; every man is a piece of the continent, a part of the main. . . . Any man's death diminishes me, because I am involved in mankind. . . ." Today the bell tolls throughout the world for those who died seeking recognition, freedom and a rightful place in the community of a free world.

". . . and therefore never send to know for whom the bell tolls; it tolls for thee."

Palm Sunday

JOHN 12:12–13

On the next day much people that were come to the feast, when they heard that Jesus was coming to Jerusalem,

Took branches of palm trees, and went forth to meet him, and cried, Hosanna: Blessed is the King of Israel that cometh in the name of the Lord.

Under all skies today the festival of the palms holds sway. The cry of Palm Sunday everywhere is: "Blessed is he that cometh in the name of the Lord." Even in the muzzled church of Russia the palms are firm, a faith that an atheistic state can never kill.

Even in the segregated areas of massacre and bloodshed in the Union of South Africa, the palms cry out that God will triumph.

Palm Sunday is the proclamation that banished truth is not vanquished truth.

It declares that truth crushed to the earth shall rise again and error will die among its own interpreters.

Harriet Beecher Stowe, the author of *Uncle Tom's Cabin,* was presented to Queen Victoria in 1856, and the Queen gave her a pair of gold bracelets. One was marked 1833, the date slavery was abolished in England, the other was bare. Victoria said: "When your country sets free the slaves you can put the date on it." Harriet Beecher Stowe thought within her heart that the day would not come in her lifetime when she could engrave that other bracelet. But one night she stood before a great mass meeting celebrating the emancipation of the slaves. She stretched out both her arms, and on them were the golden bracelets, one marked 1833, and the other now inscribed 1863. And she cried out, "The longer I live, the more I am persuaded that what ought to happen will happen."

What ought to happen will happen.

This is Palm Sunday. Live if you want to with the pessimism of day by day, but why not live as I do, with the optimism that century in and century out, "God does march on"?

The palms point to the realities of the universe: that there are laws not necessarily of man, which cannot be broken; great causes which are inevitable and invincible; great words of human speech—truth, justice, goodness, beauty and brotherhood—which are everlasting.

> Speak, history! Who are life's victors?
> Unroll thy long annals and say,
> Are they those whom the world call the victors, who
>   won the success of day?
> The martyrs, or Nero?
> The Spartans or the Persians?
> Socrates or his judges?
> Pilate or Christ?
>   —WILLIAM WETMORE STORY

A few hours after the palms, Pilate appealed to a power that seemed to be final: the might of the Empire.

But Jesus stood before him, proclaiming by his regal silence the hollowness of pomp, the pretense of pride, the ashes of ambition, the vanity of material power, the disillusionment of fame, the deception of wealth.

Pilate could appeal to a power which seemed to be final —the power of the state. Jesus could only appeal to a power which seemed to be no power at all—the power of the spirit.

And what does history say—that is, the history of the immediate hours—Pilate triumphed!

This is what always happens when Pilate encounters Christ. In any given twenty-four hours the sword always conquers the spirit. Truth and right are no match for centurions and battalions. Do you remember when Lenin was asked about the power of the Pope? He replied with the question: "How many divisions has he?"

I can remember the last time I saw Paris. I stood in the Invalides, before the red porphyry tomb of Napoleon, who waded through blood to a throne.

But looking up over his tomb, I saw hanging from the wall the uplifted form of the world's great Redeemer hanging from a cross. I remember the quotation of the Roman Emperor: "Thou has conquered, O Galilean."

Once more I looked down at Napoleon and up at the cross, and I remembered the words of Napoleon spoken on Saint Helena: "Charlemagne, Alexander and I built great empires, but they were founded on force and have crumbled away. But Jesus of Nazareth founded his Kingdom on love. There are millions today that would die for him."

Hitler stood at that tomb, after the Germans captured Paris, and prophesied that his kingdom would last a thousand years.

Look beyond Pilate today and see the crucified Jesus, and realize that with his naked, pierced hands he lifted the gates of empires off their hinges, turned the streams of the centuries into new channels, and has governed the years with the power of his love.

Christianity began not as an ivory tower of escape, not as an opiate for life's pains, but as a great adventure.

Discipleship with the Jesus of Palm Sunday has always been costly. It takes courage to begin it, and strength to continue it.

Too many have taken this religion, which began as and must continue to be a revolution, and turned it into a refuge. But the "Lone Rider" of Palm Sunday says: "He that findeth his life shall lose it; and he that loseth his life for my sake, shall find it." (Matthew 10:39)

It may be that in our personal lives we must go on past Pilate to a Calvary. Our own personal Calvary.

It may be that we must mount our cross without knowing whether it will bring us shame or fame.

But I stand here today to proclaim that Palm Sunday says that he who is against God carries his own death sentence.

The sacredness of the individual is against it.

The stars in their courses are against it.

God is against it.

Palm Sunday forever proclaims that faith is a risk and a gamble. Absolute certainty can never be faith.

By faith Abraham took a chance with God. He went out not knowing whither he went.

By faith Moses took the risk of doing what God wanted him to do rather than settle down in the certain ease of the stale luxuries of Egypt. Then, with nothing more than a mass of slaves, he dashed for freedom and found a promised land.

Ah, we sit back today and talk about our democratic faith, and we do not realize the fight that people had to wage that this would become an America.

That this would be the Harlem that it is.

That this would be the church that it is.

And that you would be the you that you are.

"In the End
... as It Began to Dawn"

A SERMON FOR EASTER

MATTHEW 28:1-8

In the end of the sabbath, as it began to dawn toward the first day of the week, came Mary Magdalene and the other Mary to see the sepulchre.

And, behold, there was a great earthquake: for the angel of the Lord descended from heaven, and came and rolled back the stone from the door, and sat upon it.

His countenance was like lightning, and his raiment white as snow:

And for fear of him the keepers did shake, and became as dead men.

And the angel answered and said unto the women, Fear not ye: for I know that ye seek Jesus, which was crucified.

He is not here: for he is risen, as he said. Come, see the place where the Lord lay.

And go quickly, and tell his disciples that he is risen from the dead; and, behold, he goeth before you into Galilee; there shall ye see him: lo, I have told you.

And they departed quickly from the sepulchre with fear and great joy; and did run to bring his disciples word.

History is filled with great moments of transition. Moments when an era comes to an end and another one begins. But all such transitional periods are not of necessity periods of progress. There can and have been periods of retrogression.

The Middle Ages, for instance, was the end of an era of Light and the beginning of an era of Darkness, and that's why it is also called the "Dark Ages."

The next transitional period was the Renaissance, when man came from out of the darkness of the Middle Ages into a rebirth, a *renaissance* of light.

Of all the great transitional periods of history none equals that which we celebrate today.

Easter marks the dawn of a new day. The dark confusion of the Old Testament's four thousand years of man's search for God came to an end. This was the day that prophets had foretold—this was the moment toward which the religious history of man had marched. This was the triumphant moment of God being revealed in all His fullness as the God of Love and Light and Life. It was the end of an era and the beginning of a dawn.

It was dawn for Mary Magdalene and the other Mary.

It was dawn for the Angel of the Lord who rolled back the stone, and his countenance was like lightning.

It was dawn for the keepers of the grave, who did shake and become as dead men.

It was dawn for the eleven disciples, who went away into Galilee into a mountain.

It was dawn when they saw Him and Jesus said, "All power is given unto me in heaven and in earth. . . . and lo, I am with you alway, even unto the end of the world." (Matthew 28:18–20)

It was the dawn of a new day when the two men at the tomb said, "Why seek ye the living among the dead?" (Luke 24:5)

It was the dawn of a new day when Peter rose and ran into the sepulcher and departed, wondering in himself of that which had come to pass.

It was a dawn of a new day when disciples walked toward a village called Emmaus and had their hearts burned within them.

It was the dawn of a new day when the doors were shut because the disciples were afraid of the Jews and Jesus came and stood in the midst of them and said, "Peace be unto you." (John 20:19)

It was the end of an era for skepticism, cynicism and all doubt when Jesus said, "Reach hither thy finger, and behold my hands; and reach hither thy hand, and thrust it into my side; and be not faithless, but believing." (John 20:27) And all the forces of doubt vanished and the dawn broke, crying, "My Lord, my God!"

It was the dawn of a new day of faith when on the Sea of Tiberia, Simon Peter, Thomas, Daniel and the sons of Zebedee were fishing, and Jesus appeared and said, "Children, have ye any meat? . . . Cast the net on the right side of the ship, and ye shall find!" (John 21:5–6)

It was the dawn of a new day of leadership when, as the disciples dined, Jesus said to Simon Peter, son of Jonas, "Lovest thou me? . . . Feed my sheep." (John 21:17)

It was the dawn of a new day of inspired writing when

the disciple who loved Jesus best, sweeping on to the end of his gospel, wrote finally: "And there are also many other things which Jesus did, the which, if they should be written every one, I suppose that even the world itself could not contain the books that should be written." (John 21:25)

It was the dawn of a new day of power when Jesus said, "But ye shall receive power, after that the Holy Ghost is come upon you: and ye shall be witnesses unto me . . ." (Acts 1:8)

It was the dawn of a new day of faith when the two men dressed in white said, "Ye men of Galilee, why stand ye gazing up into heaven? this same Jesus . . . shall so come in like manner . . ." (Acts 1:11)

It was the dawn of a new day for unity when one hundred twenty, led by Peter, James, John, Andrew, Philip, Thomas, Bartholomew, Matthew, James, Simon and Judas, gathered in an upper room and suddenly there came a sound from heaven as of a rushing mighty wind: "they were all filled with the Holy Ghost . . ." (Acts 4:31)

It was the dawn of a new day of conversion when Saul was on his way to Damascus and heard a voice crying, "Saul, Saul, why persecutest thou Me?" "Who art thou?" "I am Jesus!" "What wilt Thou have me to do?" "Arise, and go . . ." (Acts 9:4–6)

It was, finally, the dawn of a new day when the disciple John, now old, was in the spirit on the Lord's day and heard behind him a great voice as of a trumpet saying:

> I am Alpha and Omega, the beginning and the ending . . . the first and the last . . .
> And I turned to see the voice that spake with me. And being turned, I saw seven golden candlesticks;
> And in the midst of the seven candlesticks one like unto the Son of man, clothed with a garment down to the foot, and girt about the paps with a golden girdle.
> His head and his hairs were white like wool, as white as snow; and his eyes were as a flame of fire;

And his feet like unto fine brass, as if they burned in a furnace; and his voice as the sound of many waters.

And he had in his right hand seven stars: and out of his mouth went a sharp two-edged sword: and his countenance was as the sun shineth in his strength.

And when I saw him, I fell at his feet as dead. And he laid his right hand upon me, saying unto me, Fear not; I am the first and the last . . . (Revelation 1:8–17)

If the idea of the Kingdom of God is the answer to the riddle of our historical existence, then it must be called the meaning, the fulfillment and the unity of history.

"This Thing"—Jesus!

LUKE 2:15

And it came to pass, as the angels were gone away from them into heaven, the shepherds said one to another, Let us now go even unto Bethlehem, and see *this thing* which is come to pass, which the Lord hath made known unto us.

It seemed to me almost blasphemous to call the birth of Jesus "this thing." So I scoured through every translation: the American Revised Version, Twentieth Century New Testament, Goodspeed's, Moffatt's and Weymouth.

I then checked the various commentaries and I came up with a remarkable fact—without the slightest change of jot or title, they all translated this particular phrase identically: "this thing."

When one ponders the actual event, one is at a loss to put down on paper just what "this thing" is.

It could not have been recorded as one would record the birth of any child—even though it were the child of a king or president.

What was "this thing" through their eyes?

They saw with their actual eyes the first revelation of God in the history of man.

Prophets had been preparing the way. Intellectuals had been forecasting the event.

Scientists such as the astronomers had calculated through the appearance of a new constellation or the fusing of several that something would happen that never happened before.

> For unto us a child is born, unto us a son is given: and the government shall be upon his shoulder; and his name shall be called Wonderful, Counsellor, The mighty God, The everlasting Father, The Prince of Peace. (Isaiah 9:6)

Until "this thing" had happened, the word of God was only something unrevealed in the flesh but revealed in the spirit.

> In the beginning was the Word, and the Word was with God, and the Word was God.
> The same was in the beginning with God.
> All things were made by him; and without him was not any thing made that was made.
> In him was life; and the life was the light of men.
> And the light shineth in darkness; and the darkness comprehended it not. . . .
> He was in the world, and the world was made by him, and the world knew him not.
> He came unto his own, and his own received him not.
> "But as many as received him, to them gave he power to become the sons of God, even to them that believe on his name . . .
> And the Word was made flesh, and dwelt among us, (and we beheld his glory, the glory as of the only begotten of the Father,) full of grace and truth. (John 1:1–5, 10–12, 14)

They saw the greatest revelation of man: humanity and deity combined; Son of Man and Son of God, combining the finite and the infinite, the moral and the divine, the terrestrial and the celestial.

Therefore, He won acclaim even from His enemies. Pilate had to wash his hands and say, "I find no fault with Him."

He was physically perfect, "the fairest among ten thousand."

He was mentally perfect. As a child, He confounded the scribes and Pharisees.

He was aesthetically perfect, the Lily of the Valley.

His personality was so dynamic "that the common people heard him gladly." (Mark 12:37)

"This thing" was earth's greatest teacher.

His language was simple, rarely more than two syllables. His talks were short and to the point.

He taught as one in a laboratory, using deeds with the people to prove the thesis of His sermons.

When they were hungry, He fed five thousand.

When they were sick, He healed them.

His arguments were infallible.

Jesus antedated the most radical philosophy of today, Communism, by 1,900 years:

> And all that believed were together, and had all things common.
>
> And sold their possessions and goods, and parted them to all men, as every man had need. (Acts 2:44–45)

Only that philosophy, the message of Jesus, was based on God, goodness, love and nonviolence.

His authority was so complete that He was able to state with the divine sanction of God Himself that "no man cometh unto the Father," except through Him. (John 14:6)

"This thing" is the world Savior. Many religions came and went before Jesus, and many have come and gone since. But out of all the world's contemporary living religions, Jesus continues as the only Savior for all men; of all classes; of all times; of all races; of all creeds; of all nations.

"Whosoever let him come unto me."

Therefore no one can practice Christianity for whites only and still call it Christianity.

"This thing" was the Savior of the entire world—not of any particular group.

"This thing" was the only One and is the only One with the right to be sovereign of the world. From time immemorial men have dreamed of world conquest—Genghis Khan, Alexander the Great, the Caesars, Saladin the Turk, Napoleon, The Kaiser, Hitler—but they all failed.

No man can be king of kings and lord of lords except "this thing," Jesus Christ, the Son of Man, the Son of God.

Let's Give Up
Our Own Prejudices

JULY 3, 1960

GALATIANS 3:28

There is neither Jew nor Greek, there is neither bond nor free, there is neither male nor female: for ye are all one in Christ Jesus.

One of Washington's correspondents, James Reston, in a column in *The New York Times*'s editorial page, June 22, 1960, asked: "What Kind of Prejudice Are You For?" In it he says: "There is an increasingly bitter note in Senator Lyndon Johnson's campaign for the Presidency . . . for he is being rejected for the Democratic nomination because of prejudices he does not share. . . . ironically, this is coming from the North, which is always complaining about the regional prejudice of the South. . . . What are we against—all prejudices, or just Southern prejudices?"

On this Fourth of July weekend, Mr. Reston's editorial causes me as a Northerner and a Christian clergyman to pause and really ask myself: "What kind of prejudice am I for?"

As we celebrate today, the words stand before us: "We hold these truths to be self-evident, that all men are created equal."

Is not this what the minorities are fighting for? Must we not be willing to give that which we want others to give us?

Our teen-age "sit-in" strikers in the South are finding many white Southern students marching with them side by side. The prejudice which the Negro and the Northerner have against the Southerner is mainly in the heart and mind of the older Negro.

If the older Negro retains his prejudice and our "sit-in" strikers continue to register impacts on an interracial basis, then we may discover that most of our radicals next year will be moderates and our NAACP leaders will be Uncle Toms.

In other words, we, as Northerners and Christians, have got to get rid of our prejudices too, and the time is now.

I have been preaching during the past years that America needs the maturity of the free Negro to lead the way out of the suburbs of mediocrity into the centers of excellence where America can stand once again with strength.

But no Negro is free who is not free from prejudice. And no Negro is mature who does not rise above racialism and regionalism.

There is a rank hypocrisy in the North, and we all know it. The progress report issued by Dr. Theobald, Superintendent of Schools in New York City, indicates very clearly that the number of segregated schools in New York City, six years after the Supreme Court decision, have multiplied.

How dare we therefore judge all people on a blanket basis just because of accidental birth—being born in the South.

Suppose that judgment had been applied to Justice Hugo Black, a former member of the Ku Klux Klan. The Negro would have lost his best friend on the U.S. Supreme Court.

Suppose that judgment had been applied to Federal Judge Waties of Charleston, South Carolina. The Negro would have lost his best friend on the Federal District Bench.

Suppose that judgment had been applied to Homer Price Rainey, former Chancellor at the University of Texas; Dr. Frank Graham, former President of the University of North Carolina; authoress Lillian Smith of Georgia; Ralph McGill of the Atlanta *Constitution,* and other white Southerners long committed to the cause of freedom?

I appeal to you today, as a Northerner and as a Christian, that all prejudice must go now, including the prejudice that you have.

I am not endorsing Lyndon Johnson for the nomination

of President of the United States on the Democratic ticket. My candidates were Hubert Humphrey and G. Mennen Williams and Stuart Symington, and only Symington is left.

But I do want to say this firmly, emphatically and un-equivocally: Any Negro who automatically dismisses Lyndon Johnson because of the accident of birth automatically qualifies himself as an immature captive Negro, and a captive of his own prejudices.

I am not going to accept anyone as President of the United States just because he was born in the North, and I am not going to reject anyone for the Presidency of the United States just because he was born in the South.

Lyndon Johnson is the only leader that the U.S. Senate has had in eighty-two years, Republican or Democrat, to effect the passage of a civil rights bill, in 1957 and again in 1960.

Mark you, Lyndon Johnson brought the 1957 bill to a vote despite the fact that the outstanding Presidential candidate, Senator John F. Kennedy of Massachusetts, voted to send that bill back to Mississippi Senator Eastland's committee to be killed.

Let us not forget that when the Southerners issued their manifesto, it was Lyndon Johnson who led the vast majority of the members from Texas away from the Southern Manifesto and refused to sign it, thus proving where he stood.

That was a long time before there was any thought in his mind of the Presidency.

We Northerners and we Christians would take a great step forward if we let America know that we are not going to reject Lyndon Johnson because of where he was born, and that if Lyndon Johnson does get the nomination he will be accepta-ble.

This is a test of your own Christianity and if you rise to the heights you will be putting the reactionary segregationists of the South squarely on the spot so that all Americans, North-

erners and Southerners, will know that they alone are the immature people.

Let us not be captives of our own prejudices.

Let us not be brainwashed anymore by anyone, including ourselves.

Let us always remember and live by Paul's words:
"There is neither Jew nor Greek, there is neither bond nor free,
there is neither male nor female . . ." (Galatians 3:28)

For we, Northerner and Southerner, black and white, are
all one in Christ Jesus.

A New Frontier
of Faith

GENESIS 41:33

Now therefore let Pharaoh look out a man discreet and
wise, and set him over the land of Egypt.

This 1960 election was the first national poll taken on the issues of religious and regional prejudice.

The election proved the spiritual and emotional maturity of the American people and of the Negro people in particular.

A new frontier of faith was opened.

As I crisscrossed the country, speaking in thirty-four cities in fifteen states, using the full facilities of television and radio in every city, being questioned at press conferences, holding breakfast and luncheon meetings with over 1,800 clergymen, there were two issues that never faded from the campaign: (1) The Roman Catholic religion of President-elect John F. Kennedy, and (2) the region in which Vice-President-elect Lyndon Johnson was born and lived.

Except for the issue of color, the whole ferment of American prejudice was wrapped up in the Democratic candidates. The Republican candidates were safe—good, white, Anglo-Saxon Protestants.

The 1960 election can in time prove to be much more important than the placing of John Kennedy in the White House, because it was the first time a poll on prejudice had been taken.

Once before, America voted on the issue of Catholicism, in 1928, when Al Smith ran, but the issue of prohibition was also involved then. Furthermore, there was not the accompanying prejudice at that time against the Vice-Presidential candidate.

So we find prejudice was defeated by the American people on November 8, 1960.

True, it was defeated by a razor-edge margin, but it was defeated. Except for the farm belt, the election was a national cross section of the feelings of American people—and this is important.

Until November 8 the opinion-makers of America sat behind their desks and said: "Protestants won't accept a Catholic; Northerners won't accept a Southerner; Negroes won't vote for either; and so on. People don't like Jews; white people don't like Negroes; Negroes hate whites; Northerners and Southerners will never get together; ad nauseam.

But for the first time the people had a chance to state their views.

And the people showed, as is so often true, that the opinion-makers were wrong.

No more shall American people listen to the men behind the desks.

No more shall we allow the progress of brotherhood in our country to be enmeshed in the clichés and platitudes of yesterday's hate-mongers. And having disposed of the issue of religious and regional prejudice, let us proceed in our political life with the Jewish and Negro questions.

The state of Michigan has successively and successfully run two Negro candidates for statewide positions.

On November 8, the Auditor General of Michigan was elected overwhelmingly by the people. Therefore it's high time that the political overlords of New York State place on the ballot in forthcoming elections for citywide and statewide positions Negro men and women who are qualified—and the number who are qualified are legion.

It is important at the next national conventions that candidates of the Jewish faith be considered.

There is no reason why the Republicans shouldn't run a Jacob Javits for Vice-President and the Democrats an Abraham Ribicoff.

I particularly want to applaud the spiritual maturity of the Negro people, a vastly predominant Protestant group. The Negro was told by the opinion-makers that he would never be able to vote for a Catholic or a man from Dixie.

Faced with party platforms, which were somewhat similar, and a rugged Protestant faith, a Negro voter did pause for a while. But when the emotional appeals had been carefully sifted, the Negro, North and South, voted three to one for a Catholic and a man from Texas.

Why? The chairman of the Republican National Committee, Senator Morton, said that the Negro elected the Kennedy-Johnson ticket.

I will not say this.

All I will say is that if some of us had not worked as we did, the razor-edge margin of victory would have been a razor-edge margin of defeat.

The Negro voted for deeds above the emotional appeals.

He voted because Lyndon Johnson from Texas refused to sign the Southern Manifesto against the 1954 Supreme Court decision and because as the undisputed leader of the Senate he gave this nation its first civil rights bill in eighty-two years—the 1957 Civil Rights Bill.

The Negro voted for John Kennedy because in September Kennedy gave $100,000 to bring four hundred African students here when the Administration at the last minute welshed on its promises.

In October he arranged a truce between the police department and the mayor and the sit-in strikers in Atlanta, Georgia, allowing a month for them to work out a rough situation, and just before the campaign he was able with his brother to obtain the release of Martin Luther King.

This election is now a challenge to our fellow Roman Catholics.

First, if there is any anti-Protestant or anti-Negro prejudice on the part of our fellow Roman Catholics, it should be dropped now. They must realize that the anti-Catholic filth that was spewed by the hate-mongers came from a relatively small group and was even repudiated by Baptist Texas.

Second, they must not try to make religious capital out of the election of a Roman Catholic as President of the United States, but must proceed with the business of the building of the kingdom of God on earth as it is in heaven.

Third, the Roman Catholic Church is now on trial; this is not fair, but it nevertheless is true. The slightest unintentional error, word or statement could hurt race and religious relations seriously for the rest of this generation. It is therefore important that we Protestants do not hastily judge any such statements, but it is also mandatory that the hierarchy of the Roman Catholic Church see that no provocations take place.

Fourth, the Roman Catholic Church must not try to use any pressure on President-elect John F. Kennedy. As he has told me, and as he told this nation Saturday night on television: "I will not yield to any pressurers . . . I will be the President of the United States . . . So help me God!"

We stand today upon the threshold of an unparalleled opportunity, for black and white, Jew and Gentile, Protestant and Catholic, to walk together across new frontiers into a great era of brotherhood.

"Ye Are Not Your Own"

I CORINTHIANS 6:19–20

What? know ye not that your body is the temple of the Holy Ghost which is in you, which ye have of God, and ye are not your own?

For ye are bought with a price: therefore glorify God in your body, and in your spirit, which are God's.

I speak today as the minister of this historic church, and as one of the community leaders, and in my capacity as chairman of the Committee on Education and Labor in the House of Representatives of the United States Congress, which, in the language of President Kennedy, did more in 1962 for education than any other committee in the history of the republic.

New York City today stands on the threshold of a crisis —a crisis that will test men's hearts, minds, souls and spirits. Under the leadership of the Rev. Milton Galamison, and under the direction of the director of the Freedom March on Washington, Bayard Rustin, the boycott of schools begins tomorrow morning.

I wish to state unequivocally, as I have stated before, that I am in back of Rev. Galamison and the school boycott 100 percent.

Let me begin by speaking as the man in charge of the education of this nation in the House of Representatives. Regardless of how fine school buildings may be, how dedicated and educated the teachers may be, you can never have good education without integration.

So, purely on an educational basis, this boycott is mandatory. Speaking again as one of the leaders of Harlem, this boycott is necessary to separate the men from the boys. To separate the men and women of character from the Uncle Toms.

As Rev. Galamison said, "We cannot turn back."

Two hours from Washington, D.C., the Ku Klux Klan is marching in Cambridge, Maryland. Gloria Richardson has appealed to the Department of Justice, and they are investigating.

On this Tuesday night I will be in Cambridge, Maryland, speaking for Gloria Richardson.

Every day this week I will be on the floor of Congress fighting to hold the line, that we may be able to pass the most comprehensive civil rights bill in the history of this nation, with teeth in it.

All across the South black men and women are marching: in Atlanta, Georgia; in Hattiesburg, Mississippi.

It is my hope and prayer that this school boycott, which begins tomorrow, shall become national.

And finally, I speak as the minister of this church. I tell you in the language of Paul:

> What? know ye not that your body is the temple of the Holy Ghost which is in you, which ye have of God, and ye are not your own?
>
> For ye are bought with a price: therefore glorify God in your body, and in your spirit, which are God's. (I Corinthians 6:19–20)

The final voice in the life of our community, in the life of our home, in the life of our church, even in our own life, is not the voice of our conscience, not the voice of the President, not the voice of the mayor, or of the Board of Education, nor the voice of the minister of the church.

The final voice is, always has been, always will be, the voice of God: Ye are not your own.

The rich man thought he had the final voice when he said, "Soul, take thine ease, eat, drink, and be merry."

The final voice was: "Thou fool, this night thy soul shall be required of thee: then whose shall those things be, which thou hast provided?" (Luke 12:20)

When you recognize that the final voice is the voice of God in your life, there comes to you not only a sense of character, knowing that whate'er befalls you, God doeth all things well, but there comes to you a sense of peace and inner security.

You know then that no man, however powerful, nor any group of men can pass the ultimate judgment on nations, races and human beings. Sometimes we may be like David when he said:

> But as for me, my feet were almost gone; my steps had well-nigh slipped. For I was envious at the foolish, when I saw the prosperity of the wicked. (Psalms 73:2–3)

And on and on he goes, talking about their pride, their fatness, their oppression, and their lofty way of speaking and even setting their mouths against the heavens. And he couldn't understand it.

He said, "It was too painful for me when I wanted to know about this. Until one day I went into the house of God, and then I understood their end, that God did set them in slippery places, and did cast them down in destruction.

"Then I understood their end."

Since the final voice is God, the ultimate motive of duty is to God. We have loved ones, friends, connections, wealth, position, and our natural impulses urge us to follow our own selfishness, our own course.

Our immediate interests lie in following it. Our so-called friends say we ought to follow it. But one day there comes a conviction, and a clear call of God to another way. I appeal to you that when this comes, do not deny that call, for ye are not your own.

The knowledge that we are not our own gives us courage in these difficult days, in this world of so many voices claiming to have the final word.

It is soul-soothing, and mind-easing, and spirit-strengthening to know that the final voice is in God.

The voices of the state seethingly rise above all else, and all over this seething world men obey the voice of the state. The final word will yet come from Him who rules the earth, the heavens and the seas, and stars in orbit that have never been seen.

The voice of science speaks objectively from the throne of proved fact, and says we have the final word concerning the things of the intellect and of the earth.

In these days the voice of finance, industry, capitalism, money may seem to have the final word. But the final voice has not yet spoken: the voice of Him who holds the world in the hollow of His hand, where the cattle upon a thousand hills belong to Him; the voice of Him who lives upon the horizon, where everything is within His vision.

In these void days, the voice of dynamic progress may claim to have the final word. The voice of Him to whom a thousand years are but a day has yet to be heard.

In these days the voice of force, the tread of marching men, the searing of the skies, the intercontinental missiles may seem to have the final say. But the voice has not yet been heard from Him who hath put down the mighty and exalted the humble.

In these days the voice of white blacklash may claim to have the final word, although it is speaking rapidly with less authority.

But the final word will one day be spoken by Him in whom there is no east or west, who out of one blood made the entire world, who is classless and raceless.

No, ye are not your own, for ye are bought with a price.

The Courage to Repent

REVELATION 2:5

Remember therefore from whence thou art fallen, and repent, and do the first works; or else I will come unto thee quickly, and will remove thy candlestick out of his place, except thou repent.

ACTS 2:38

Then Peter said unto them, Repent, and be baptized every one of you in the name of Jesus Christ for the remission of sins, and ye shall receive the gift of the Holy Ghost.

The world's largest monument, in Geneva, Switzerland, is erected to the memory of Michael Servetus, executed by John Calvin. He held different views of the Trinity and baptism, and was put to death as a heretic. The monument was set up by Calvin's followers as a monument of repentance.

One of the hardest things in the world is to confess a wrongdoing.

We always give a much more kindly treatment to our own moral pleasures than we do to those of others. If there is one fact which is obvious about today's world, it is the lack of the courage of repentance. In spite of all the suffering, disaster, ruthlessness and wars in this century, no monument stands in any city, nor can it be discerned in the consciousness of the people of any nation.

Self-righteousness is the characteristic of life today. Russia on one side says "We are the peacemakers, you are the warmongers." On the other side we say the same. A New York newspaper editorial recently concluded by saying, "The judgments of free mankind are true and righteous *altogether*."

The Christian interpretation of events is that the past lives in the present.

Past evils are the cause of present chaos.

Unless the past is dealt with, chaos will continue to reign in individual life, group life and national life.

What is repentance?

It starts with looking back to the evil thoughts and deeds of yesterday and saying, "I have sinned against heaven and in Thy sight, O God."

People say that "man may repent, but how can a nation?" I reply that public opinion, which is the mood of the masses, can be fashioned into either self-righteousness or humility and sorrow. This is the trouble of our world since World War II—an absence of any sense of common guilt. The world wants peace without repentance.

The tragedy of Siloam lay in the collapse of its power; eighteen men were killed and the people said the suffering was due to sin. The disciples came to Jesus and raised the question: ". . . think ye that they were sinners above all men?" Christ answered, "I tell you, Nay: but, except ye repent, ye shall all likewise perish." (Luke 13:4–5)

On another occasion, Jesus forgave when He knew a person had truly repented.

> Jesus went unto the mount of Olives.
>
> And early in the morning he came again into the temple, and all the people came unto him; and he sat down, and taught them.
>
> And the scribes and Pharisees brought unto him a woman taken in adultery; and when they had set her in the midst,
>
> They say unto him, Master, this woman was taken in adultery, in the very act.
>
> Now Moses in the law commanded us, that such should be stoned: but what sayest thou?
>
> This they said, tempting him, that they might have to accuse him. But Jesus stooped down, and with his finger wrote on the ground, as though he heard them not.
>
> So when they continued asking him, he lifted up himself, and said unto them, He that is without sin among you, let him first cast a stone at her.
>
> And again he stooped down, and wrote on the ground.
>
> And they which heard it, being convicted by their own conscience, went out one by one, beginning at the eldest,

even unto the last: and Jesus was left alone, and the woman standing in the midst.

When Jesus had lifted up himself, and saw none but the woman, he said unto her, Woman where are those thine accusers? hath no man condemned thee?

She said, No man, Lord. And Jesus said unto her, Neither do I condemn thee: go, and sin no more. (John 8:1–11)

Second, the courage of repentance means a determination to turn away from that which we have been doing, and a driving desire to set out in a new direction.

What has happened to our world since World War II? The guns still stand, the bombs are still poised, the planes are still fueled. Money is still being appropriated for the same tensions, the same arguments and the same policies; therefore the world knows no peace.

In our personal lives the same problems confront us. We have moods in which we regret the past, we have a sense of sincere godly sorrow for sin, but we fail to take the next step. We cannot find strength to break with the past.

Oftimes we are sorry for what we did, but we do not repent.

New beginnings are tremendously difficult.

Past attitudes and actions become deeply imbedded.

Habits, thoughts and emotions establish their own patterns.

We are like Nicodemus when he asked Jesus, "How can a man be born when he is old?" (John 3:4)

The old English schoolmaster in *Good-bye Mr. Chips* raised the question: "Can a man in mid-life start again?"

The answer to such questions in the teachings of Jesus is: New beginnings are always possible!

Repentance makes possible forgiveness and forgiveness sets new forces flowing. This results in peace of heart, which is the only peace, in the last analysis.

The whole Christian faith is built on the reality of a new beginning.

It begins with the tremendous fact of the birth of Jesus Christ, the Son of God, which represents the supreme new beginning of all history: the numbering of the years changed, the calendar refashioned and mankind given a fresh start.

From here on, new beginnings in man and new beginnings in nations could be expected. "Therefore if any man *be* in Christ, *he is* a new creature: old things are passed away; behold all things are become new." Paul said this (2 Corinthians 5:17) and he should know, for it happened to him.

I dreamed a dream. I walked through the world and saw the endless monuments to the great military heroes of yesterday, shrines recording the great national achievements of the past. I came upon a new monument—a monument of Repentance.

In South Africa there was one set up and it had the word "SHARPEVILLE" on it.

In Russia there was one set up in Moscow and had the word "HUNGARY" on it.

In England it had the word "SUEZ."

In Germany it had the words "SIX MILLION JEWS."

In France the word "ALGERIA."

In America it had the word "NEGRO."

Santa Claus versus Jesus Christ

ACTS 20:35

I have shewed you all things, how that so labouring ye ought to support the weak, and to remember the words of the Lord Jesus, how he said, It is more blessed to give than to receive.

ROMANS 6:23

For the wages of sin is death; but the gift of God is eternal life through Jesus Christ our Lord.

Louis Lomax told his children the other day, "There will be no Christmas presents for you this year because there are six little ones sleeping the eternal sleep in the red clay of Birmingham, Alabama."

From that came the idea posed by a man, James Baldwin, that this year those of us who are Christians celebrate a Christian Christmas.

I have always been against commercialism of any kind in the field of Christianity. I am against the commercial intent of Mother's Day, because it was originally invented by the florists and candy shops to put forward their wares. I am against Father's Day for the same reason. I am against the commercialism of Easter.

You can recall the many times that I have stood here and castigated people for putting so much money to their outer selves and coming to church on Easter Sunday without a thought of their inner selves. The same has been my view for Christmas. I stopped mailing "Christmas cards" several years ago. I do mail a message—one that has nothing to do with Santa Claus or presents, but one that begs for prayers and for a world of peace and goodwill.

Just last year, I sent a letter to 109 relatives asking them under no circumstances to give me any present, nor my two sons a present, but that they would be welcome at my home during Christmas for a gathering together.

And I can state that the Christmas that we spent together last year with this large family was one which everyone agreed was one of the finest they had ever attended.

Something dramatic must be done to keep alive the memory of those six children bombed in Birmingham. And I can think of nothing more dramatic than to emphasize Jesus Christ this year and to forget Santa Claus.

Santa Claus, after all, is "a legendary character." *The Columbia Encyclopedia* traces him to the fourth century, when there was a Bishop Nicholas in Asia Minor, who later on was sainted by the Roman Catholic Church.

The people of Greece and Italy adopted Saint Nicholas as their patron saint for little boys and celebrated his feast day on December 6.

In Holland it became the custom to give little boys presents on December 6 in honor of Saint Nicholas, whose name the Dutch pronounced "Santa Claus."

According to *The Columbia Encyclopedia,* the English people appropriated this legendary character, moved him up to the day of Jesus' birth, and that is how Santa Claus was born.

It is interesting to note that Anglican England took a Roman Catholic saint in order to commercialize Christmas.

Yet when you leave the Anglo-Saxon world of Christianity and go into the Mediterranean and Latin American world of Christianity, where the population is 98 percent Roman Catholic, there is no Santa Claus. Christmas is celebrated as it should be—seriously, enjoyably, and above all spiritually.

Here in New York City our newspapers have been filled with reports, year after year, of the drunken brawls that take place on Christmas Eve in our skyscrapers, where office parties last from morning until night. This is what we call "Santa Claus."

So I say this year, let's lift up Jesus Christ and forget Santa Claus.

Give the jolly fat fellow a vacation.

He has absolutely nothing whatsoever to do with the birth of our Lord and Savior Jesus Christ; absolutely nothing whatsoever to do with Christianity.

Peace on earth and goodwill do not come from him, a red-suited man ringing a bell, but from the red blood of Jesus Christ hanging on a cross.

Santa Claus versus Jesus Christ.

What is Jesus?

The birth of a baby that split history in half—B.C. and A.D.

The contribution of a new and permanent moral philosophy.

The bringing of God to man and man to God.

The establishment of an eternal church.

The dynamic outreach of the church.

The breaking down of all barriers of class, and of nations, and of race.

A Savior who is: ageless . . . timeless . . . spaceless . . . raceless.

> And I, if I be lifted up from the earth, will draw all men unto me. (John 12:32)

Why I Am a Christian

OCTOBER 2, 1955

JOHN 14:6

I am the way, the truth, and the life: no man cometh unto the Father, but by me.

In the history of humanity there never has been a tribe of men without some form of religion. The Bushmen of central Australia, the Indians of Patagonia cherished some beliefs in the spirit world and engaged in some kind of worship.

The oldest monuments of civilized man as shown in the pyramids of Egypt and the early Veda scriptures of India indicate religious practices.

Every religion does many things for the religious individual and usually to society: it provides the individual with added power and satisfaction; it helps him to bear the troubles of life; it offers a solution to the problem of evil; it improves the quality of his present life, and offers the hope of a better life; it outlines an ideal society; it sets forth a working plan of salvation.

Today there are eleven living religions: Hinduism, the religion of divine imminence and a hereditary graded social structure; Sikhism, a religion of one God, with doctrines taken from both the Hindu and Moslem faiths; Jainism, the religion of asceticism; Buddhism, the religion of disciples of the one true God; Confucianism, the religion of social propriety; Taoism, the religion of the divine way; Shintoism, the religion of emperor worship; Judaism, the religion of obedience to the righteous God; Zoroastrianism, the religion of struggle along with a good but limited God against the evil forces inherent in the world; Islam, or Muhammadanism, the religion of the all-sufficient world potentate; and Christianity, the religion of the love of man as revealed in Jesus Christ.

What are the general points of similarity and dissimilarity among these religions?

Belief in one supreme being

This was originally repudiated by Buddhism, but later the founder was worshiped. Confucianism is limited to the worship of only one person in China, the Emperor, and that only once a year, December 22. It encourages the common people to worship the spirits both of nature and of ancestors.

Hinduism believes in one supreme impersonal cosmic being named Brahma, to be meditated upon, not to be worshiped. The popular form of Hinduism is notoriously polytheistic, and is characterized by the actual worship of many gods.

A genuine definite belief in the worship of one supreme cosmic power by all people can be found in only four religions—Judaism, Christianity, Muhammadanism and Sikhism—but none of them present a God who in His own character is self-sacrificingly seeking the redemption of the world, who is historically represented by a person of that same moral character. Christianity's doctrine of monotheism has the highest possible moral content, a holy, loving, heavenly Father who actively seeks the welfare, trust, obedience, cooperation, love of all men.

The claim of divine incarnation

In Hinduism, every object may be regarded as a temporary manifestation, or embodiment, or impersonation, of the impersonal, nonmoral, eternal Brahma, through the high-caste Brahman priests, who are especially venerated. In addition there are several other gods, from nine to twenty-one, and there is worship of animals. Yet none of these beings are represented as morally perfect, nor are they represented as manifestations of one supreme personal cosmic deity.

In Buddhism, Buddha came to be regarded as a kind of incarnation, yet only one of twenty-four incarnate Buddhas, with the twenty-fifth still to come.

In Christianity there is a distinctive and central teaching concerning Jesus Christ as the unique incarnation of the Word of God, preeminently manifested in the historic person, on the ground that his moral character perfectly represents the character and purpose of the invisible holy God: ". . . he that hath seen me hath seen the Father . . ." (John 14:9) "And the word was made flesh, and dwelt among us . . ." (John 1:14)

The claim of supernatural origin of the founder

Only three other religions we are considering have such a theory.

Buddha was the firstborn child of a queen, forty-five years old, who had a prophetic dream of his birth.

Confucius was carried in his mother's womb for seventy-two years—or for eighty-one years—according to different traditions.

Zoroaster was born of an unmarried young woman fifteen years of age, who was "glorified."

The claim of divine revelation

Every one of the eleven living religions in the world has made the claim of possessing divinely saving truth. Moreover, every Christian may recognize certain specific revelations of truth which God has made in each of the other systems of religion, whereby (Acts 14:17) "he left not himself without witness" anywhere among the communities of the world.

Not a single major teaching of any religion is lacking in Christianity. But in Christianity only are all the major teachings of the eleven living religions included, harmonized and supplemented by a high revelation that: the supreme power in the world is a perfect person; that He may best be conceived of and lived with as a Father; that he has been adequately presented by His Son, Jesus Christ; that the supreme satisfaction of every human being consists in loving obedience to Him and in loving service to his fellow man.

The claim of an inspired scripture

Not one of the twelve dead religions possessed anything which might be called a canon of sacred scripture. But all of the eleven living religions do possess definite sets of documents which are regarded as conveying unique divine truths that need to be known for salvation. Only the Veda and the Koran are supposed to be verbally inspired and literally infallible by the same authority set forth for the Bible.

Of the sacred scriptures of Hinduism, the one most highly esteemed is the Bhagavad-Gita. This is the only literature in all Hinduism that offers universal salvation to all sinners (Chapter 4, Verse 36), even to women and the lower caste; however, it reaffirms very specifically (Chapter 4, Verse 13; Chapter 18, Verse 43) the rigid caste systems of Hinduism.

Indeed the new deity, Krishna, says "the four castes were created by me."

The report of miracles wrought

All of the eleven living religions report, usually in connection with the life of their founders, wonderful events of great religious experiences. Many reported miracles of the Bible may be paralleled with the sacred scriptures of other religions, but no historic person other than Jesus has ever been reported to have risen shortly after his death and burial and to have continued his customary influence upon his disciples.

The principle of the Golden Rule

This teaching concerning the proper method of dealing with other people has been approximated as a summary rule of right conduct in eight different systems of religion and philosophy. However, Jesus is the only one who stated the principle of the Golden Rule positively and universally, not negatively as a warning to abstain from misbehavior. Jesus is the only one who Himself applied that principle with consistent self-sacrifice, even toward his enemies. Jesus is the only one who based this universal rule of human conduct upon the character of universal conduct of God Himself:

> Love your enemies, bless them that curse you, do good to them that hate you, and pray for them which despitefully use you, and persecute you;
> That ye may be the children of your Father which is in heaven: for he maketh his sun to rise on the evil and on the good, and sendeth rain on the just and on the unjust. (Matthew 5:44–45)

Recognition of an especially sacred community

Every religion in the world teaches that there is or should be some particular group of people regarded as peculiarly sacred. Buddhism thus regards only those who are gathered together into a special order. Women, however, are regarded as inherently inferior. Hinduism teaches that its whole caste system is a sacred institution, the upper caste being the most holy. Muhammadanism cuts clean across all ideas of hereditary status and social superiority, and says, "They who believe, and have bled and have fought, these only shall be next kin of each other." Muhammad taught that those infidels who do not literally submit themselves to Allah and become Muslims deserve only to be exterminated.

Christianity alone teaches that all human society has a sacred moral character, and that every individual, every nation, should be brought lovingly into the comprehensive brotherhood of humanity under the universal thought "whosoever will come after me, let him deny himself, and take up his cross, and follow me." (Mark 8:34)

The hope of a universal religion

The idea of a universal religion does not occur in the sacred scriptures of the three nationalist religions, those of India, China and Japan—Hinduism, Confucianism and Shintoism. The only religions that aim for universality are Buddhism, Christianity and Muhammadanism. Buddhism has not expanded in the world. Muhammadanism remains the only formidable rival to Christianity as a universal religion, but it excludes half its own adult adherents—women—from participation in the privileges and responsibilities of their religion.

Christianity alone, of all the religions in the world, teaches that all human beings are children of a common Father, and that all Christians should engage in loving self-sacrifice, religious testimony and systematic service unto the whole world.

The hopes and fears of a future life

Hinduism and Buddhism teach that the present life is so sadly marred by suffering that it is really not worth continuing. All four of the religions that originated in India teach the doctrine of transmigration by the power of the impersonal law that a person's soul becomes reincarnate after death in some other earthly value according to his conduct of his present life.

Confucianism offers a future without hope of heaven, without fear of hell, without consequences of any kind.

Muhammad glowingly pictured a paradise filled with sensual delights for the pious and a hell of perpetual agony for the unbelieving.

Christianity teaches that there shall be a sure and just judgment for all people! Good people will enter into the increasing joy of closer fellowship with God, the wicked will suffer the terrible consequences of being separated from God, which they have already chosen. The glorious hope of progressive spiritual life comes only to those who have a loving attitude toward all people in this world.

What are the radical dissimilarities of Christianity?

In the first place, the character of God is as a loving heavenly Father.

Eight religions do not mention this at all. Three only touch on it. The New Testament is the only document, the only religious scripture of the world which teaches that the supreme deity is a universal heavenly Father.

In the second place, the character of the founder is the Son of God and the brother of all men.

Jesus Christ alone is reported as having had a consistent God-consciousness, a consistent character Himself and a consistent program for His religion.

He was the son of man and the Son of God.

He grew in the flesh yet participated in the eternal.

He is the elder brother of all men, pioneer of our fate, captain of our salvation, unequaled by any other person who has ever lived upon earth, yet possessed of qualities and personalities which all persons should possess. Indeed, "by the fellowship of His Grace we attain under the perfection of His character."

In the third place, there is the presence of a divine universal holy spirit.

Christianity is the only religion that teaches us a doctrine of great practical as well as scriptural importance: that there is at work in the world a divine universal holy spirit indwelling, teaching, suggesting, reprimanding, inspiring, transforming, available for all individuals who will open their hearts to this divine inner influence.

In God there is something eternal, best known as "The Father."

In God there is something historic in the life of Jesus Christ, "The Son of God."

In God there is something progressive, which leads us forward under the guidance of "The Holy Spirit."

The problems of evil and salvation for me personally, the thing that makes me a follower of the Jesus way is the keenness of its analysis of evil and the appropriate salvation which it offers.

The Jains are concerned with physical evil, yet they are not encouraged by their religion to enjoy good health, but practice asceticism.

The Buddhists are concerned chiefly with emotional evil, yet they are not encouraged to live a more abundant personal and social life, rather to suppress individuality altogether.

The Hindus look for salvation through Yoga or "union" with God, but they look for it at the expense of the loss of their personality, the absolute and final cessation of personal existence.

Jesus, however, came preaching, "I am come that they might have life, and that they might have it more abundantly." (John 10:10)

Taoism says evil is something to be ignored.

Hinduism says that evil is ultimately unreal because it is illusory.

Muhammadanism says evil is relatively unreal because it is arbitrary; the only evil in the world are the non-Muslims.

Confucianism says there is not much evil in the world; man is inherently good.

But Christianity says that evil is a terrible and widespread fact in life. Each individual is directly responsible for choosing evil rather than good. The fundamental evil is any selfish use of our God-given free will, with its resultant injury to our personality. All individuals are liable to evil and actually do sin against God, against other persons and against their own best self.

But, thanks be unto God, salvation is available to all—women as well as men, the lowest class as well as the highest, the believers and nonbelievers.

> Take my yoke upon you, and learn of me. (Matthew 11:29)

> . . . whosoever believeth in him should not perish, but have eternal life. (John 3:15)

> God so loved the world, that he gave his only begotten Son, that whosoever believeth in him should not perish, but have everlasting life. (John 3:16)

He is the propitiation of our sins, we are reconciled by His death, we are saved by His glorified life, we are justified by His blood. He gave His blood as a ransom for many. He shed His blood for the remission of sins. As He said one day to His disciples, "without me ye can do nothing." (John 15:5)

So today I am a Christian. This is not intolerance but Positive Protestantism. I belong to His church, which was established upon a rock, and the gates of hell shall not prevail against it.

I hear the call of Jesus ringing in my ear:

> Go ye therefore, and teach all nations, baptizing them . . . and, lo, I am with you alway . . . (Matthew 28:19–20)

Yes, I know there is a tendency in certain sections of Christianity to deviate from the vision, faith and dedication of the founders; to lack the ideal of personal fellowship with God; to shirk the responsibilities which accompany the privileges of being children of God; to overemphasize theology instead of maintaining the founders' emphasis on moral conduct; to be domineering instead of following the founders' teachings and example of service; and to divide, because of questions of belief, worship and organization instead of uniting on the basis of brotherly love.

Nevertheless, I follow that One who once said, "he that hath seen me hath seen the Father . . ." (John 14:9)

In thirty-seven verses Jesus spoke of Himself as being sent by God.

In thirty verses He is represented as consciously fulfilling the Old Testament but also consciously superseding the phases of Judaism.

In John He is proclaimed as a co-worker with God.

In Matthew He said: His gospel would be preached to the whole world.

In Mark: He gave His life to all men and He gave it as an example for us to follow.

He is presented as the Savior of men in a variety of intimate relationships both with men and with God.

> I am the good shepherd: the good shepherd giveth his life for the sheep. (John 10:11)

> I am the door; by me if any man enter in, he shall be saved . . . (John 10:9)

> I am the true vine, and my Father is the husbandman . . . ye are the branches . . . (John 15:1, 5)

> I am the resurrection and the life: he that believeth in me, though he were dead, yet shall he live . . . (John 11:25)

> I am the way, the truth, and the life: no man cometh unto the Father, but by me. (John 14:6)

I am the bread of life: he that cometh to me shall never hunger; and he that believeth on me shall never thirst. (John 6:35)

I am come a light into the world, that whosoever believeth on me should not abide in darkness. (John 12:46)

If any man will come after me, let him deny himself, and take up his cross daily, and follow me. (Luke 9:23)

Till heaven and earth pass, one jot or one tittle shall in no wise pass from the law, till all be fulfilled. (Matthew 5:18)

The New Church

I TIMOTHY 3:15

But if I tarry long, that thou mayest know how thou oughtest to behave thyself in the house of God, which is the church of the living God, the pillar and ground of the truth.

However we may disprove Communism and hate the violence employed to further its goal, we have to admire its adherents' singlehearted devotion to their common aims. The Christian faith, above all other ideologies, is supposed to know the meaning of community solidarity—"losing oneself so that one may find oneself." But does it?

The great evil of today is materialism. Materialistic evil through its own solidarity is gobbling up much of the earth.

Part of the evil lies in "bigness."

We are living in a period where Big Business, Big Labor and Big Government are controlling our lives.

Man's constant search for liberty is in danger of ending on a note of frustration in the sea of "Bigness" in which we find ourselves.

There can be but one panacea, one ray of hope for men who would continue the search for liberty: a Third Force of all faiths, united in one church.

For this is the only hope of mankind. We must relearn Christian solidarity. We can learn this only when we are of one accord, when we are united with one another, and with Jesus Christ.

In politics, the American ideal is constructed upon the principle of a two-party system.

Theoretically, these two forces are separate and distinct

and man's search for liberty would find safety in the choice between these forces.

Actually, we are seeing a complete breakdown in our two-party system.

The confusion created by Dixiecrats in the Democratic Party and phony Northern white liberals and reactionary members of the Republican Party has compounded the ills of the Negro people and has created a vacuum which must be filled.

In this winter of our discontent, not only must man turn to the church; the church must turn to man.

The church must move into this vacuum as a Third Force, fighting an unrelenting battle for the liberty of the Negro people. Only then can the church become this new church.

I therefore call for a Third Force of all faiths; of men of God moving in a sphere of dynamic religion, not only to save men's souls, but to set these souls free from the bondage of discrimination and segregation.

There are men today who argue that politics should be kept out of the church. We are not putting politics in the church, we are putting religion into politics.

God created the church to serve as a force of good. How else can we fulfill His purpose, except by using the church to free the Negro people from that hell on earth created by men of ill will?

We must build, today, a renaissance of the church.

We must fill our churches to a point of overflowing.

We must give to our church coffers until it hurts.

We must rally behind our ministers and give them that kind of courage which can only come when they know that their flock is with them.

We must pray.

We must pray and fight and pray and fight until all of us can worship God as free men.

Martin Luther understood this mandate when he wrote:

And though this world with devils filled
Should threaten to undo us,
We will not fear, for God hath willed
His truth to triumph through us.

That is our faith.

Einstein understood the heretofore dormant power of the church when he declared:

Only the churches stood squarely across the path of Hitler's campaign for suppressing truth. I am forced to confess what I once despised, I now praise unreservedly.

The need of the hour is a church visible. Any unity too powerless to be evangelistic is irrelevant.

Invisible unity of spirit cannot be detected by the world. We can easily grow in our individual graces and denominations and still make no corporate impact upon the world.

What is our choice? Be holy first, and universal last? Or vice versa?

Here we've made our most tragic mistake: It is our opportunity to be more universal as we have opportunities.

There used to be a time when a Baptist would rather die and go through fire than worship with a Methodist. Today Protestants are joining the church nearest them, irrespective of denomination.

Unity is important today in this church.

This is marked by two great revelations:

First, He lives and because He lives we shall live also.

Second, His spirit comes to empower us when we are of one accord.

Stand alert today to preserve that accord at any cost, because the spirit of the living God shall empower His Church again.

From the ashes of a divided world will arise the New Church.

Are You the Right Size?

EPHESIANS 3:17–18

That Christ may dwell in your hearts by faith; that ye, being rooted and grounded in love,

May be able to comprehend with all saints what is the breadth, and length, and depth, and height, . . .

I want to ask you today: "Are you the right size?"

The verse which I have just read to you deals with measurements. This is very good for our day, because so much of our material world is based on accurate measurements.

There are incredible instruments today which can measure everything. I can take an electric micrometer and measure one ten thousandth of an inch. I can peek into one of the new giant telescopes and see a galaxy of stars a thousand light-years away. I can go to M.I.T. and use the new electrical computer and, by pressing buttons, solve a problem in higher mathematics that would have taken Einstein, with paper and pencil, years to do.

Here in this text, Paul gives us an ideal for the right measurements of life: "breadth, and length, and depth, and height."

We must realize that we have to be the right size in our world of survival of the fittest.

One of the laws of comparative anatomy is: "A small animal has resistance to gravity relatively ten times greater than its driving force."

That's why a fly can walk on a ceiling or a mouse can fall a thousand feet and only be slightly dazed.

Prehistoric monsters died out because they were the wrong size for biological success. So every type of animal (and that includes us) has an optimum size. Our question for this morning is: "What is the right size of mind and heart to fit our day and our world?"

I was in Buckingham Palace in England. One of my guides told me that Queen Anne of England was "the smallest person to ever sit in a large place."

Some crucial events in history have come about from small people and large places. It was the stupidity of George III of England that gave the world the American Revolution. It was the stupidity of Nicholas II, Czar of Russia, that gave the world Communism. It was the stupidity of Batista that gave Cuba the Castro revolution.

We must be the right size for our environment.

We have already changed tremendously. We are living longer than our forefathers.

Through motion pictures and television we can hear a pin drop in Europe and a bomb drop in Asia.

Do we have minds that match our eyes and our ears?

In days gone by they used to cry, "Give me men to match my mountains!"

We need the right personal measurements that we may achieve the breadth and depth and height of responsible citizenship.

Anyone who fits snugly and smugly into a small world of individual interests is the wrong size.

I call upon you this morning to take the most momentous journey in the world—from "I" to "We."

When the rich young fool purred to Jesus his self-satisfaction over his prosperity in three short sentences, he used the word "I" or "my" thirteen times. Jesus said, "Thou fool."

I sat the other day talking to a very wealthy young woman. She talked literally for hours. I couldn't get a word in. In this earth-shaking hour the important people for her were Helena Rubinstein, Elizabeth Arden, Hattie Carnegie, Emily

Post, Lilly Daché, Fanny Farmer and Betty Crocker. They are all good gals but they are too small for our world.

We need people today who are the right size to fit the globe, the only size that has any survival value.

Our world is full of shortages, and one of our most critical shortages is that of people with heads the right size to fit a globe. There used to be a time when a few people could make things happen, but now world survival demands all of us.

None of us may be a de Gaulle, a Khrushchev, a Nkrumah, or a prime minister or secretary of state, but we can be a genuine force if we keep the impact of our life on public opinion. One person with his mind made up can push a lot of folks around.

Two things are clear: First, we need thinking rather than military power to resolve our present issues.

Second, we must stop dealing with the results of Communism and start dealing with its causes. The empty promises of Communism make no appeal to well-fed Americans, but they are of tremendous appeal to the hungry, landless and hopeless millions of Asia, Africa and Latin America. We must meet the festering evils upon which it thrives.

That means material and spiritual help!

If we are to be the right size for our day, we must be tall enough to bump the sky.

When the young folks used to hear Emerson lecture at Boston, they didn't understand what he was saying half the time, but they went out with their heads "hitting the stars." That's the right height—tall enough to hit the stars. As one of my favorite hymns, "Higher Ground," declares: "I'm pressing on the upward way, new heights I'm gaining every day."

Are you big enough for God?

If anything is to grow, it needs two worlds: the "earth-plus relationship" with the sky, the sun, the rain and the wind.

We need the "God plus": "the beyond which is within."
"Beloved, now we are the sons of God . . ." (I John 3:2)
God plus weakness equals strength.
God plus one is a majority.

Christ in the Nuclear Age

JOHN 16:32–33

Behold, the hour cometh, yea, is now come, that ye shall be scattered, every man to his own, and shall leave me alone: and yet I am not alone, because the Father is with me.

These things I have spoken unto you, that in me ye might have peace. In the world ye shall have tribulation: but be of good cheer; I have overcome the world.

I believe it is the business of the preacher to say an eternal word in a contemporary setting; to say a permanent word in a changing world; to help those who enter the doors to have not only a sense of history but a sense of the age.

I know it is difficult to get a sense of the eternal in our nuclear age because of its many benefits. I should like to name four of them:

First, the nuclear age has lifted people out of the life of drudgery.

Second, the nuclear age has provided more time for leisure. What man does in work goes into his pocket. What he does in leisure time goes into his character.

Third, the nuclear age has made possible for every human being on the face of the earth the basic necessities of life for the first time since creation began.

Fourth, the nuclear age has reduced the size of the world. "Science made us neighbors. I pray to God that justice will make us friends," said Senator Borah.

Theoretically we live in one world, but in reality we are divided into nations, races, classes and neighborhoods.

What are the problems of the nuclear age?

Again may I name four:

First, it has caused people to lose their sense of timing. For one thing, just push a button and get a light or a secretary, or drop a bomb. We fail to realize that social, political and economic things are not solved by the pushing of buttons. It is a question of timing.

We have come to this moment of world leadership technically prepared and morally unprepared. We are demanding of men what only God can produce in them.

Second, we have confused our scale of values.

Most of us believe that a gadget will be invented to solve our problems and our needs.

Life begins from within; not in gadgets but in the discipline of principle, responsibility and hard work. Social and economic problems are solved by brains and character.

Third, we have lost the worth of the individual.

Mr. Jones and Mr. Smith walk down the street, bump into each other and tip their hats. Mr. Jones and Mr. Smith drive down the street and hit each other with their cars. Look at the difference.

There is a dimension in man which machinery cannot measure, interpret, understand or provide.

Fourth, we are tempted to misread the meaning of the universe. God made this world to be a home dedicated to brotherhood, to be a cathedral dedicated to worship, to be a school dedicated to learning. This we must have: interpreted by a higher light than any machine can produce, directed by a stronger control than anything mechanical can provide—and handled by a greater power than man can generate.

What is the answer of Jesus to us in this nuclear age?

1. He is the source of man's moral and spiritual strength. Let us contrast efficiency with sufficiency:

Efficiency speaks of skill—sufficiency is the power to be skilled.

Efficiency means tools—sufficiency, the strength to use tools.

Efficiency practices notes—sufficiency masters the harmony.

Efficiency is the hand—sufficiency is the heart.

Efficiency builds the boat—sufficiency is the ocean to float it.

Efficiency is skill—sufficiency is culture.

Sufficiency means the fullness that deals with dimensions which machinery cannot measure, interpret, understand or provide.

Jesus is the source of man's moral and spiritual strength. He provides for power without having to become a slave to any machine: "My grace is sufficient for thee." (II Corinthians 12:9)

2. He furnishes a quality. The secret of what man can do is underneath what he can be, and Jesus is interested in what he can be. He enables us to be our best so that we may do our best: "Till thou hast bound me fast I am not free."

3. The champion of personality, He has given to the world forgiveness.

For example: You might cut the bark off a tree. Nature would give it a chance to heal. If I cut my finger, nature would give it a chance to heal. But if my mind or soul is wounded and hurt, I would be lost if it were not for the forgiveness of Jesus.

By His Grace, He gives us strength.

By His forgiveness, He gives us quality.

By His Cross, He gives us character.

When the last gadget is gone, when the clock is stopped, and nuclear electronics can discover no new horizons, be sure of this:

Nothing Christlike will ever perish!

Every Christlike thought

Every Christlike deed

Every Christlike word

Every Christlike service
Every Christlike work and
Every Christlike life will sustain us for eternity.
"Be of good cheer; I have overcome the world."

Stop Worrying

PSALMS 37:1–7

Fret not thyself because of evildoers, neither be thou envious against the workers of iniquity.

For they shall soon be cut down like the grass, and wither as the green herb.

Trust in the Lord, and do good; so shalt thou dwell in the land, and verily thou shalt be fed.

Delight thyself also in the Lord; and he shall give thee the desires of thine heart.

Commit thy way unto the Lord; trust also in him; and he shall bring it to pass.

And he shall bring forth thy righteousness as the light, and thy judgment as the noonday.

Rest in the Lord, and wait patiently for him: fret not thyself because of him who prospereth in his way, because of the man who bringeth wicked devices to pass.

Ulcers are the mark of modern man.

When you are always busy and have no goal; when you are always anxious and are frustrated; when you are always fretfully stirring, your life can achieve no purpose.

There are always more words to be spoken.

Always more books to be read.

Always more jobs to be done.

Always more blows to be struck.

But today we have redefined progress. We are considered successful today when we are nervous, frustrated, disagreeable, stomach out of order or gall bladder being operated on. In order to counteract this modern tempo we must realize that nobody is ever free from fret. Because there is too much unfinished business.

Some of us fret because we choose the wrong roads, the wrong hills to climb, the wrong goals to seek.

We struggle too much with status symbols—dollars, clothes, houses, cars, impressive friends.

Jesus said: "Take no thought . . . seek ye first. . . ." (Matthew 6:25–33)

So realize that life depends upon quality and not quantity.

You do not have to read everything in order to be educated. You do not have to know everything to be wise. You do not have to see everything in order to be happy. You do not have to do everything in order to have a rich life of fulfillment.

But Americans feel that the effectiveness of living depends upon the quantity of conspicuous consumption.

Right now, in order for the whole world to live effectively and comfortably, we do not need to see, to have, to do, to know a single new thing.

The creature comforts for our entire world are available this moment as I speak.

Our problem is that we cannot project our present knowledge.

"Fret not thyself because of evildoers" because there are more people in this world on your side than you realize.

Out of the treasury of wisdom of the seers who have passed there comes a saying: "Whoever works for good will never be unemployed."

And I add to this: ". . . and will never be ineffective."

Ignore the few with their bitterness, snobbery, false pride, false education, self-importance. Because it is the labor of the earnest and the humble that is never in vain.

There is no such thing as a common task.

This world could easily get along without me, but I think of the chaos if the so-called common people stopped working.

The best portion of our lives are the little, meaningless, unremembered acts of kindness and love.

". . . Inasmuch as ye have done *it* unto one of the least of these my brethren, ye have done *it* unto me." (Matthew 25:40)

There would be no fret or, in the language of the street, no "sweat," if we knew God's power, God's providence—and trusted in them.

Many things in the world we call luck are not accidents.

Many tragedies that come to us are but a preparation for a better life.

Many things that are seemingly superficial are real.

The scorn of today can be the thunderous applause of tomorrow.

The loss of a battle does not mean defeat.

To sum it all up, it is man's judgment versus God's, and the weakness of God is stronger than the strength of man.

When the tides of the fretful break with a roar upon the beaches of our souls, we can find peace if we believe "it is well, it is well, with my soul."

Paul said: "For whether we live, we live unto the Lord; and whether we die, we die unto the Lord: whether we live therefore, or die, we are the Lord's." (Romans 14:8)

Here are people who never fretted:

Dickens, frail and lonely as a child, wrote such literary masterpieces as *A Christmas Carol, The Pickwick Papers* and *David Copperfield.*

Lincoln was depressed and could not come to grips with his problems, but when the crisis came, he found strength.

Fannie Crosby, who never got out of a wheelchair, composed the immortal hymn "Blessed Assurance."

To sum it all up:

There is a power in this world which is not ours. There is a will which is not our own. There is a victory that does not depend on us. God lives and as Psalms 46:1–5 declares is "our refuge and strength, a very present help in trouble.

"Therefore will not we fear, though the earth be removed, and though the mountains be carried into the midst of the sea . . .

"There is a river, the streams whereof shall make glad the city of God . . .

"God is in the midst of her; she shall not be moved . . ."

Man's Debt to God

PSALMS 116:12–13

What shall I render unto the Lord for all his benefits toward me?

I will take the cup of salvation, and call upon the name of the Lord.

The founding fathers of the First Continental Congress did not bestow upon the American citizen the right to freedom; they merely recorded the fact that his Creator originally endowed him with that inalienable right. Liberty, therefore, is of God, not of men.

Nor is this a peculiar possession of America. Its roots are deep in human nature everywhere. There are even countries in the world—alas, too many—that regard regimentation as the only way of escape from economic and social slavery.

Love of liberty runs deep. There is nothing new in its promises of freedom, whether they come from Nasser or Nehru.

But freedom is not reached by a single bound; there is an unavoidable technique. First, knowledge gained; then knowledge applied; then, and only then, freedom. Never has this been better expressed than "ye shall know the truth, and the truth shall make you free."

At first cringing before the mysteries of matter, force and life, man has gradually risen to his Creator's challenge to take dominion over the physical world about him.

As he came to know, he became free. Only as far and as fast as he understood was he liberated.

Freedom from an impoverished physical existence (from famine, cold, privation and discomfort) has been attained as rapidly as the knowledge of the earth's materials and forces have produced food, fuel, shelter, clothing, light and power.

We have gone a long way from the caveman to the steam-heated air-conditioned modern home of stone, brick, lumber, steel and glass.

A far cry from the precarious food sources of the savage to the menu of this day.

A far cry from the toil of hand labor, and the glow of starlight and lightning flashes, to the harnessed electricity of today. Great is the story of man's emancipation from danger, darkness, drudgery and discomfort. Man has broken metes and boundaries of time and space only through expanding knowledge.

The vibrations of man's puny voice were smothered by the heavy encircling atmosphere to a few rods or furlongs, but today, with the speed of light, the words of a president fall simultaneously upon millions of listening ears in every corner of forty-eight states, to the insular possessions, the isles of the sea and the distant continents.

The cruising range originally was but a few square miles; it was gradually extended by domesticated animals, by cattle, by sail, by sea, by electricity, by steam, by gas explosions, until now we can literally, as written in Psalms 139:9, "take the wings of the morning, and dwell in the uttermost parts of the sea."

Descartes once claimed we could be free from an infinity of maladies of body and mind if we had sufficient knowledge of their causes and of the remedies nature provided.

This was astonishing three hundred years ago, but trite today, for we have received emancipation from the imprisonment of disease and deformity, suffering and death by means of expanding knowledge.

The progressive freedom is no less sharply illustrated in this social and economic world about us. Knowledge, which has freed us from famine and pestilence, will also free us from the sword as we create social and economic, national and international laws and forces.

However men may differ on analysis of causes on proposed plans and on current experimentations, mankind is practically unanimous in its determination that it must be freed from poverty, insecurity, fear; and that mindless, heartless, soul-less economic laws shall no longer enslave.

Finally, therefore, "ye shall know the truth, and the truth shall make you free." These two things are God's gift to us: Truth and Freedom.

I would like to present a few deductions concerning these gifts.

1. The authority of truth is absolute.

It is by decree of God, not by plebiscite of man. It is a birthright no more than a right; it is a duty.

"For we cannot but speak the things which we have seen and heard." (Acts 4:20)

Freedom at times may partake somewhat of the nature of a social contract, but basically it is with God and its tides cannot be swept back by the petty brooms of kings or legislatures.

2. The creature, freedom, is not greater than the Creator of truth.

This rules out any idea of freedom as caprice or the unrestricted right to do as one pleases. The process of freeing will be as slow or as fast as the process of learning.

3. Freedom cannot be bestowed or conferred.

It can only be attained or earned.

God Himself cannot grant or even force freedom upon the ignorant or the self-willed.

4. Only through the law can freedom be obtained.

Never apart from it or against it.

Liberty is not for the lawless.

The laws I am talking about are the laws of God.

We are witnessing the decreasing immaturity of the Southern white in the face of the increasing maturity of the Southern Negro because of respect for the law of God.

5. Absolute freedom is impossible.

It is as impossible to say that I will have complete freedom but no discipline, as it is to say I will always relax and never contract my muscles. You will find the freedom wherewith Jesus Christ has set you free only as you accept the discipline of God.

6. The highest freedom consists in identification with the law of God.

His is written on the heart.

The rule of the soul.

It operates from within outward, rather than from without inward.

Freedom is an internal achievement rather than an external adjustment.

The freest man in the world is the man who is geared to the eternal and in harmony with God. He then—and only he—is free to do as he pleases, because he always wants to please—to do the things that are pleasing in the sight of God.

What are the Truths of God?

1. This is His world.
2. I am His child.
3. His purpose will triumph.
4. Vengeance is His.

The earth is the Lord's and the fulness thereof; the world, and they that dwell therein. (Psalms 24:1)

Walking under a Cloud

DECEMBER 13, 1953

EXODUS 40:34–38

Then a cloud covered the tent of the congregation, and the glory of the Lord filled the tabernacle.

And Moses was not able to enter into the tent of the congregation, because the cloud abode thereon, and the glory of the Lord filled the tabernacle.

And when the cloud was taken up from over the tabernacle, the children of Israel went onward in all their journeys:

But if the cloud were not taken up, then they journeyed not till the day that it was taken up.

For the cloud of the Lord was upon the tabernacle by day, and fire was on it by night, in the sight of all the house of Israel, throughout all their journeys.

Never since the Dred Scott Decision has the United States Supreme Court had before it as momentous a problem as the one placed before it this week.

The abolition of segregation in the public school system of America is more than a national problem, more than a racial problem, more than a political problem, more even than a problem of the Constitution. It is a moral problem which will directly shape the ethical future of the entire world.

I applaud to the highest the daring leadership of President Eisenhower in suggesting an international pooling of atomic energy resources. May God give him the strength and wisdom to carry this program to its completion.

But I state, and state most emphatically, that even the successful completion of the Eisenhower program for world atomic energy must be unsuccessful as long as the people of the earth know that 15 million American citizens are walking under the legalized cloud of segregation. In the eyes of the world, we are in the same category as the Union of South Africa and its doctrine of apartheid.

We have turned the clouds of segregation into a guiding symbol.

A cloud is a symbol of an oncoming storm. Most people regard sunny skies as the prophets of mercy. The people of Israel, walking under a cloud of deprivation, oppression, conquerors, knew that.

"Ye fearful saints, fresh courage take; these clouds ye so much dread are filled with mercy and soon shall break with blessings on thy heads."

Secondly, a cloud indicates a divine presence. God is always closer when you need him more.

The majority of the Negro people know that—not to our bitter regret but to our increasing joy. Where would we be as a race today had it not been for the fact that when we walked under every cloud, God walked with us?

Many political, social, educational and economic advantages have come to the Negro people from being forced to live under a cloud and under stress.

However, this could not have happened if it had not been for God's presence, which has turned our "mourning" into gladness.

Finally, to walk under a cloud is a guarantee that one day you will walk in the light. For ". . . where sin abounded, grace did much more abound . . ." (Romans 5:20)

Even in the darkness there is light. "And the light shineth in darkness; and the darkness comprehended it not." (John 1:5)

The thing that has sustained Negro people has been their followship of Jesus Christ.

"I am the light of the world: he that followeth me shall not walk in darkness, but shall have the light of life." (John 8:12)

In the midst of darkness, the Bible gives us the flashes of prophetic illumination which light our way.

No sky ever remains permanently cloudy.

You shall not always walk under a cloud—as a race, as a world, as individuals.

> The people that walked in darkness have seen a great light: they that dwell in the land of the shadow of death, upon them hath the light shined. . . .

For unto us a child is born, unto us a son is given: and the government shall be upon his shoulder: and his name shall be called Wonderful, Counsellor, The mighty God, The everlasting Father, The Prince of Peace.

Of the increase of his government and peace there shall be no end . . . (Isaiah 9:2, 6–7)

Are you walking today under a cloud—of fear? of insecurity? of loneliness? of bitterness? of hopelessness? of heartbreak? of frustration? of tension? of aches? of inferiority?

"Come unto me, all ye that . . . are heavy laden, and I will give you rest." (Matthew 11:28)

Democracy and Religion

PSALMS 133:1

Behold, how good and how pleasant it is for brethren to dwell together in unity!

This is the hour of crisis in modern times—the hour toward which the prophets of doom have been pointing. It is not an hour of crisis because of the manifest evils: bickerings, creedal quarrels, denominationalism, ritualism, clericalism; it is due from the enemies without—our professed friends.

Democracy is by far the best political system under which man lives, but there is no guarantee that it shall continue as such.

The only guarantee of a continuance is the improvement of democracy.

This can be done only by Christian leadership. Christian leadership is most effective when we go out and preach and teach outside of the church.

There is no inalienable right to govern, but the human spirit does demand to be governed with justice. Politics, like preaching, should be the function only of those best fitted to perform its duties. Today, democracy places too much power in the hands of a voting public largely incompetent, ethically insensitive; places the unfit in office while others, of ability, are excluded because of the party system; legislates en masse, and thereby offers too many "pork barrels."

I call today for the men and women of the church to commit themselves, without reservation, to the democratic ideal but to a revision of those elements within the democratic system which thwart attainment.

First, the church must never relinquish its spiritual task of fellowship, personal living, acceptance of social obligation, realistic faith in men and a sense of a divine dependency.

Second, however, the church should lay more stress upon the participation in politics as a religious vocation. This should take the place of the emphasis of past years on being a missionary.

Third, the church must preach nonviolence.

Fourth, the church should arouse its members to nonpartisan political action on any issue where the principle of respect for personality is at stake—child labor, sharecroppers, civil rights, housing, public health, the rights of workers.

Fifth, the church should resist vigorously the exalting of the power of the state above the Christian conscience. Whenever the church compromises its spiritual message, it undermines its redemptive power.

Sixth, the church should lay upon its members a sense of their responsibility to be a nucleus from which a new democracy can be built.

Seventh, the church needs to make reason and revelation the approach to the truth. Without reason there is no knowledge of how to act in civic affairs. Without revelation one sees little to ask for.

What are the barriers to realization of our ideals?

First, within the church there are: denominationalism; class cleavage; racial exclusiveness; economic domination by large givers; power cliques.

Second, there is a tendency of clergy and pew to estimate their own success by the kind of church they belong to. All persons are children of God.

Third, spiritual pride interferes. Too many people limit their words and deeds to what brings the greatest response from their peers rather than from the common folks: The sheep are not being fed. We need therefore to stand firm on those things which cannot be shaken by class and creed, denominationalism and race.

What can unite us? Five things: God, Jesus, Prayer, Man and the Cross.

God—What one thinks about God will determine one's attitude toward self, neighbor, vocation, earthly future and eternal destiny.

Jesus—the revealer of God and the redeemer of man. It was not so much what He taught as what He demonstrated. We cannot help ourselves. God, through Jesus, imparts new vitality through forgiveness of sin and the lifting of its burdens.

Prayer—A vital belief in prayer has faded from modern thought; the intellectual foundation has been undermined by doubt in the existence of a personal God who cares. There must always stand before us the witness of the Christian gospels to the loving care of God, the witness of ourselves to the personal power of faith as we know it through Jesus Christ.

Man—"It is He that has made us and not we ourselves." We are chosen of God as creatures of infinite worth, for we are transient and eternal.

The Cross—This unites through suffering and love. This is God's way of turning sacrifice into joy—for the joy that was set before Him endured the Cross.

This is the way of reconciling man to self and to one another. This is God's way of bringing triumph out of defeat.

The Injustice of Justice

MAY 23, 1960

ECCLESIASTES 5:8

If thou seest the oppression of the poor, and violent perverting of judgment and justice in a province, marvel not at the matter: for he that is higher than the highest regardeth; and there be higher than they.

Next week I will introduce in the House of Representatives several bills aimed at abolishing capital punishment within the United States of America.

The first bill will abolish capital punishment in the District of Columbia.

The second, in the armed forces.

The third, in the federal judicial system.

And the fourth will establish the mechanism for the adoption of a Constitutional amendment to abolish it within the fifty states.

Why am I going to do this?

The execution of Caryl Chessman brought public opinion of the United States to a new low. This could only have been surpassed by an incident such as the "U-2" espionage flights over Soviet Russia. I have consulted the man whom I consider the nation's leading criminal lawyer, Edward Bennett Williams. I have used the material brought together by Ernest Havemann, in an article in this month's issue of *Reader's Digest*. And I will quote from the article by Herbert Wechsler, former Assistant Attorney General of the United States, now Professor of Law at Columbia University, an outstanding authority on criminal law.

Mr. Williams:

Caryl Chessman's twelve years in "death row" have underscored the inhumanity, the injustice, and the inequality of

capital punishment. Inhuman, because its deterrent effects
are now recognized as a myth; unjust, because it leaves no
remedy for a mistake; unequal, because it is exacted almost
exclusively of the poor and the ignorant. In short, it is a
relic of the barbarous days when the Mosaic Code demanded "An Eye for an Eye."

Mr. Havemann:

Nine states and forty foreign countries have abolished the
death penalty! Lawmakers have decided that society loses
far more than it gains when it puts a man to death. The
law is not infallible. It is always possible that an innocent
man may be executed. In the case of Charles Bernstein, in
the District of Columbia, he was minutes away from the
electric chair when a messenger rushed in with the news
that his sentence had been commuted to life. If that messenger had been caught in traffic, Bernstein would have died.
Two years later, the police found positive proof that Bernstein was innocent of the murder and he was released.

In California, two men named Thomas and McCain were
tried for killing a woman during a holdup. Thomas was
poor and defended by a Court-appointed lawyer who let
him plead guilty before a notoriously strict judge. Nothing
was said in Court about his previous good record. He was
executed! McCain had a good lawyer; pleaded "not guilty";
took the case before a jury . . . he got a life sentence.
Both for the same crime!

Mr. Wechsler:

In 1950, 4,300 prisoners were sent to State and Federal
Penitentiaries for murder. Half of these convictions may
have rested upon conduct that could have been punished
by death. But that year there were just 82 executions in
the United States. The issue, therefore, is not whether we
should put to death every man who commits a capital crime,
but the issue is whether a small, and random, selection of
the people convicted of murder ought to be executed for the
rest, or imprisoned?

Evidence clearly shows that execution does not act as a deterrent to capital crime.

The District of Columbia has mandatory death sentences. If this were an act to deter crime, then the District of Columbia should have the lowest murder rate.

The truth of it is the District of Columbia has the highest in this country!

The nine states that have abolished capital punishment, according to the FBI, have a lower homicide rate than the neighboring states which retain the death penalty.

The death penalty has a bad effect on the administration of justice. A trial in which a human life is at stake inevitably becomes a morbid and sensational affair. The public is aroused in such a way that justice is not easily obtained.

Except in rare instances, the serious offenses are committed by those suffering from mental illness, or who are impulsive in nature, and are not acts of the criminal.

When the death sentence is removed, more convictions are possible with fewer delays.

Unequal application of the law takes place because those executed usually are the poor, the ignorant, or the unfortunate.

Warden Duffy of San Quentin said in his book: "Seldom is a person of means executed!" Warden Lawes, of Sing Sing, who supervised the execution of 150 men, said the majority of them had been too poor to hire a lawyer, and were defended by counsel appointed by the court. A high-priced Texas lawyer has defended 200 murderers, and only one of them has been executed!

The great Clarence Darrow once observed: "Only the poor are put to death."

In 1958, the majority of the defendants executed in this country were poor Negroes. As Ed Williams says: "A penalty which has been virtually abolished for white men with money, ought to be abolished for everybody."

Society is amply protected by a sentence of life imprisonment.

Society has an important interest in salvaging a life, however bad the record may be.

Criminals spared from death, who are released after a term of years, have better records on the whole than released prisoners in general.

For example: California statistics show that of the 342 prisoners convicted of first-degree murder, and paroled between 1945 and 1954, only nine returned to prison on a felony conviction.

Civilized society has moved forward in its concept of crime and punishment. In this decade we must move still further. The gallows, the gas chamber, the electric chair, should be relegated to our museums; to their appointed places along with the rack, the thumbscrew, the guillotine, and other discarded instruments of primitive injustice.

But what is the spiritual aspect of capital punishment?

More important than all of these excellent reasons given by learned men is the fact that no man has the right to take the life of any other man; at any time; for any reason. Except, possibly, accidentally in self-defense.

The law of God declared: "Thou shalt not kill."

Jesus restated this law of God thus:

> Ye have heard that it hath been said, An eye for an eye, and a tooth for a tooth:
> But I say unto you, That ye resist not evil: but whosoever shall smite thee on thy right cheek, turn to him the other also.
> . . . Love your enemies, bless them that curse you, do good to them that hate you, and pray for them which despitefully use you, and persecute you; (Matthew 5:38–39, 44)

The final judgment again is restated by Jesus:

Judge not, that ye be not judged.

For with what judgment ye judge: and with what measure ye mete, it shall be measured to you again. (Matthew 7:1–2)

The ultimate yardstick of Christianity: "Inasmuch ye have done *it* unto one of the least of these my brethren, ye have done *it* unto me." (Matthew 25:40)

One Must Die
for Many

JOHN 16:7

Nevertheless I tell you the truth; It is expedient for you that I go away: for if I go not away, the Comforter will not come unto you; but if I depart, I will send him unto you.

It may seem hard to start a sermon on Pentecost talking about the crucifixion of Jesus; but if you will bear with me as we move along in this discussion, maybe what I will say will bring some light to this situation.

To me, the most shocking thing about the crucifixion of Jews was the crime's encouragement by the official religious leaders of that time.

Now Caiaphas, who was the high priest, the chief, the bishop, the pope, the presiding elder, the moderator—whatever you want to call him—he summed it up for everybody else: "Now Caiaphas was he, which gave counsel to the Jews, that it was expedient that one man should die for the people." (John 18:14) In other words, it seemed better to get rid of one man than to have the people disturbed and excited.

One of the main things that the leaders of the status quo, organized society, or whatever you want to call it, always strive to do is not to upset the people nor, of course, to allow anyone else to upset them.

This is one of the most common excuses that men use to get rid of a single man.

It never seems quite the right time for a particular truth to be announced.

It's never the right time to take a particular stand.

All kinds of arguments are marshaled to show that this

sort of thing can do more harm than good just now, and we had better wait for a better time.

A man who will not wait must be bludgeoned into silence.

The argument for defying the Supreme Court is based on the assertion that we must not move too fast.

One of the most ridiculous statements in this connection was made by Congressman Frank Thompson of New Jersey when the "Powell Amendment" was passed and included in the "School Construction Bill."

He said: "The Powell Amendment is not necessary now, even in those states that have segregated schools, but which are moving with all deliberate speed."

In other words, we are always preferring generalities to concrete situations.

People talk about politics in general, just as long as no one brings up a particular political situation or candidate within one's own district.

We can talk about economics in terms of charts and trends, just as long as no one brings up the tragedy of the man next door who is out of work.

Education is kept general and dull by talking about theory.

Theology is all right, as long as it's academic.

Jesus never dealt in generalities or abstractions, but with concrete situations, the specifics.

This is the meaning of His parables.

It is the reason why His teachings have lived, and why He speaks to us today as clearly as to the people in the first century.

People are persons. The ever-present danger is that we shall always accept some idealistic position that makes it possible to sacrifice a man, or a few men, for what seems to be a great social good.

That's what the Nazis did; the Fascists; and the Communists.

To enforce conformity upon men for their own good is a betrayal of everything the gospel has taught us about the dignity of men.

We must never become so wrapped up in our church work that we forget our personal duties to each individual man.

Above all, let's remember that God works through individuals and not masses.

Progress has never come through majority action.

Progress comes when a lonely man hears God speak to him and passes His word on to the rest of us. Even though sometimes we do not hear Him gladly.

Therefore, I am against any man, or group of men, having the power to decide the life and death of a fellow human being.

I am against the Crucifixion. I am against capital punishment. But I want to point out that in the economy of God there are times when God decides that the death or persecution of one man is good for the people.

This is the whole meaning of Pentecost:

"It is expedient for you that I go away: for if I go not away, the Comforter will not come unto you . . ."

This was God's decision. The historical element in the ministry of Jesus had to come to an end. The limitations of space and time that characterized his sojourn on earth had to give way to the eternal and the universal, so that he could fulfill his promises. ". . . lo, I am with you alway, even unto the end of the world." (Matthew 28:20)

The era of the holy spirit begins with Pentecost.

The Savior of the Jews had to become everybody's Savior. This is the significance of every man's hearing in his own tongue the mighty works of God.

The holy spirit had to declare Jesus to the whole world.

The spirit had to convert the facts of history into faith.

It had to make objective history become personal history. ". . . no man can say that Jesus is the Lord, but by the Holy Ghost." (I Corinthians 12:3)

The holy spirit convicts the world because it believes not in Jesus.

The spirit works to convict the world and to acquit the believer. This is why most of us flee from even a consideration of the holy spirit, because naturally we do not want to be convicted. We reduce our responsibilities and our obligations and hope, therefore, to reduce our judgment. We avoid making decisions because if we can avoid making decisions we might not make too many wrong ones and suffer consequences.

We remain silent in controversial moments, because then we cannot be judged severely for what we say, and even less so for what we don't say.

And we keep a comfortable distance from people because we do not want to be involved in any personal way with others so that we won't be criticized or hurt.

But if we try to hinder the spirit of God from convicting us, from crucifying our own selves, then we in turn are preventing the spirit from resurrecting us.

We must take the risk of involvement to enter into life at its most demanding period.

If we do all this, then the holy spirit brings joy to our hearts.

In this same magnificent chapter Jesus said:

> A woman when she is in travail hath sorrow, because her hour has come: but as soon as she is delivered of the child, she remembereth no more the anguish, for joy that a man is born into the world.
>
> And ye now therefore have sorrow: but I will see you again, and your heart shall rejoice, and your joy no man taketh from you. (John 16:21–22)

The Whole Gospel
for the Whole World

I TIMOTHY 4:10

For therefore we both labour and suffer reproach, because we trust in the living God, who is the Saviour of all men, specially of those that believe.

As we face our world today and as we think in particular of our church theme, THE WHOLE GOSPEL FOR THE WHOLE WORLD, and apply all this to the special emphasis of this day, MEN AND MISSIONS, we must come to the first conclusion that there has been a reversal of the cultural tide.

During the nineteenth and early twentieth centuries there was tremendous political and economical and cultural expansion of Western society into all the world. Coinciding with this period was the greatest period of missionary expansion. These were expansions of basically white races into parts of the world populated by colored peoples. The fact we must face today is that that movement has been in the main halted or reversed.

The Gospel for the Whole World is no longer associated with the cultural and political powers that are in dominance. In other words, the dominating power of the world today in the vaster section and among the greater majority of the population is non-white.

Coupled with this reversal of the cultural tide has also come a reverse of the non-Christian religions. Thus Islam is definitely the greater power in the missionary field than is Christianity. Likewise there has been tremendous expansion in Buddhism and Hinduism, for instance; even among the most modern and most educated, more and more are pushing Christianity into the background. Christianity, then, we must realize, is not the only missionary religion and not even the strongest.

Another significant event in the world that we live in is the birth of what I must call a single world civilization. For years I have been associated with the World Association of Parliamentarians.

I was one of its founders and served for years as one of its vice-presidents. We were a small voice crying in the wilderness around eight or nine years ago.

Today we find that outstanding groups of people in increasing numbers are beginning to work toward a rule of law for our world rather than a rule of force, and any rule of law necessarily includes a world community of some type.

More and more the majority peoples of the earth are repudiating Western cultural and political domination, and this repudiation is forcing us to live together more and more in a one-world civilization where modern science and technology are playing an important part as a sort of social cement in bringing together the fragmented portions of our civilization.

One of the tragedies we face is that while this world of modern civilization was brought to birth within Western Christendom, Christianity itself has to a large extent failed to come to terms with its own offspring.

There is no great conflict between science and religion in those portions of the earth that are non-Christian, but to a great extent modern man in Western society has become alienated from the Christian tradition.

Since there is now developing a single world civilization, there is emerging also a single world history. For centuries vast portions of the earth and individual man himself have drifted because there has been no concept of history in the light of some belief as to the meaning of the story which is told.

People have drifted. Races have drifted. Nations have drifted.

But today there is a world history and there can only be a world history if there is some belief as to the direction in which mankind as a whole is moving, and that involves his origin as well as his destiny.

Whereas people in the past have wallowed in the pools of nonhistorical existence and waded in the rivulets and streams of tribal history, now they are beginning to move out into the single Mein Kampf of a world history.

This means the events are judged to be significant in the light of their relation to the direction of our world as a whole.

More and more nations have had to adopt a calendar in which events are reckoned on a single time scale which dates from the birth of Christ. Why?

Because Jesus Christ is the driving force of this main current of world history: A force that is drawing nations irresistibly out of their separate existence into a common world history. A force that is drawing all men out of their shells of isolation and racism into a single community of the human race. A force that has its foundations in the revelation of God through Jesus Christ.

The reign of God broke into human history in the coming of Jesus Christ and we possess a faith that it will be finally sovereign over all things.

Anybody who truly grasps at this faith immediately is capable of giving meaning to his life and to the history of mankind as a whole, and to the individual history of any other human being.

There is the danger that such a philosophy may be monopolized by a particular group to prove its own sense of history.

Second, it can and has given rise to the totalitarian state.

Third, it can lead to an individual piety which seeks to secure the status of the individual at the expense of robbing the drama of world history.

No one can achieve meaning for the history of the individual at the cost of destroying the meaning of history for the whole.

May I recommend that you take the Bible as your clue to the understanding of history. The coming of Christ into the world is the revelation of the true destiny of man and history. That coming precipitated a crisis.

Once the fact of Christ became known, life could no longer go on as before. It could not continue in the prehistoric pattern, it could not continue in the channels of mere tribal history; an irreversible change took place since the question was posed "What is man?" and this question can never be evaded.

One must accept the principles of Jesus as the true revelation of human destiny; a radical break with the powers and structures of this world.

We must meet the absolute claims of absolute authority with the absolute counterclaim that God is ALL IN ALL. History must be led to converge toward a single, final focal point—that Jesus Christ is the Savior of this world and of all that dwell therein.

In order to do this we must strip Jesus of any racial monopoly, cultural denomination, let His ideas go free into all the world, baptizing and teaching all those who will believe.

What a Day to Live in

GALATIANS 2:20

I am crucified with Christ: nevertheless I live; yet not I, but Christ liveth in me: and the life which I now live in the flesh I live by the faith of the Son of God, who loved me, and gave himself for me.

Many people around this broad, seething earth may not agree—in fact, some of them cannot agree—with our subject of today: "What a day to live in."

But for the black masses of the United States, and for those whites who are marching with them, I say this is a great day to live in. And for those of us who are Christians, I can think of no finer exultation than the great Magnificat by Mary.

> . . . My soul doth magnify the Lord,
> And my spirit hath rejoiced in God my Savior.
> For he hath regarded the low estate of his handmaiden: for, behold, from henceforth all generations shall call me blessed.
> For he that is mighty hath done to me great things; and holy *is* his name.
> And his mercy *is* on them that fear him from generation to generation.
> He hath shewed strength with the arm; he hath scattered the proud in the imagination of their hearts.
> He hath put down the mighty from their seats, and exalted them of low degree.
> He hath filled the hungry with good things; and the rich he hath sent empty away.
> He hath holpen his servant Israel, in remembrance of *his* mercy. (Luke 1:46–54)

Yes, this humble woman—living in the slums of Nazareth, out of which no good thing could come; wife of a man making substandard wages; delivering her child in the cattle trough of a cave which was used as a stable—could thank God.

Then we of this generation should look for a cause in her reasons to substantiate my thesis for "What a day to live in."

Therefore, let us think about God and His mercy to them that fit it.

It means in substance that there is nothing that the world can do against the people of God that will cause God to forget them as long as they "reverence him."

He hath scattered the proud.

The day of dictators in high places and in low places has passed. Nobody has sensed this more sensitively and completely than the black mass: that there will always be unity among men and women who are not proud and arrogant but in their humility will stand together.

He hath put down the mighty.

No person ever ruled this world for a considerable period through force and power and might and arrogance. Those who would seek to destroy the sons of God always end in self-destruction.

Not by might, not by power, but by my spirit, saith the Lord.

Let us make the world safe for what is right.

He hath exalted them of low degree.

As you go back through history, the masses that have successfully resisted power propaganda, inequality and injustice have always been of low degree.

True leadership has always come from the rank and file.

The men and women of history who have brought to this world any semblance of social progress, and substituted humanity for inhumanity, have in the main been barefoot prophets— men clad in rags, wandering in the desert, all souls proclaiming their protests from the depths of slavery.

This is our racial and religious heritage.

It has not been the mighty and the noble who have liberated mankind. It has been the Jeremiahs; the John the Baptists in the wilderness.

Paul, in writing to his friends in Corinth, sensed this when he said that God hath chosen the weak of the world to confound the mighty. In the base of the world, people are despised. God hath chosen to bring to naught the things that are. He hath filled the hungry with good things.

I try my best not to believe in a God with materialistic attributes.

"You are wrong!"

God does feed, clothe and shelter those who believe in Him.

But above all, God does fill his people who are hungry with good things that are more than the things that are material.

Jesus summed it all up when he said:

> Take no thought for your life, what ye shall eat; neither for the body, what ye shall put on.
> But rather seek ye the kingdom of God; and all these things shall be added unto you. (Luke 12:22, 31)

> . . . no good thing will he withhold from them that walk uprightly. (Psalms 84:11)

> I have been young, and now am old; yet have not seen the righteous forsaken, nor his seed begging bread. (Psalms 37:25)

> . . . the rich he hath sent empty away. (Luke 1:53)

Here we are attacking the war on poverty when the private corporations, private foundations of this nation could on a tax-free basis conduct this war and spend much more than the $1 billion that I am asking for in the bill before my committee.

The meaning of the story of the rich young ruler who

came to Jesus was not so much that Jesus told him to sell all he had, but that He told him to give it to the poor.

This is why I have always had a sense of compulsion in my preaching, because Jesus stood up that day to preach and He said:

> The spirit of the Lord is upon me, because he hath anointed me to preach the gospel to the poor; he hath sent me to heal the broken-hearted, to preach deliverance to the captives, and recovering of sight to the blind, to set at liberty them that are bruised . . . (Luke 4:18)

This is the theme of the Black Revolution. Where are our big ministers in this revolution?

Jesus helps His people. Mary said He hath helped His servant Israel. Oh, yes, look back through all the pages of history, and whenever the crises have seemed so dark that everything was lost, there came a Prince of Peace with healing in His wings.

In the darkest hours of human history, when all hope had seemed to vanish, God stepped in and helped His people.

Sometimes they were making bricks without straw down in Egyptland.

Sometimes they were hungry prophets being fed with manna.

Sometimes they were thirsty people in the wilderness.

Sometimes they were a raggedy, pitiful group with nothing in their hands, marching before the great walls of the great city of Jericho.

Sometimes they were three teen-agers being cast into a fiery furnace.

Sometimes they were men being thrown into the cage with lions.

Sometimes it was a Gandhi in India; a Kagawa in Japan;

a Marcus Garvey for Africa; brown leaders in Asia; Latin Americans in South America.

Sometimes it was a black soul in slavery in the United States of America.

Sometimes it was a group of students in Princess Anne County, Maryland.

Sometimes it was a Jesus Christ hanging on a cross.

I will say of the Lord, He is my refuge and my fortress: my God; in him will I trust. (Psalms 91:2)

. . . they that wait upon the Lord shall renew their strength; they shall mount up with wings as eagles; they shall run, and not be weary; and they shall walk, and not faint. (Isaiah 40:31)

Mother's Day

PROVERBS 31:10, 27–28

Who can find a virtuous woman? for her price is far above rubies. . . .

She looketh well to the ways of her household, and eateth not the bread of idleness.

Her children arise up, and call her blessed; her husband also, and he praiseth her.

MATTHEW 12:48–50

But he answered and said unto him that told him, Who is my mother? and who are my brethren?

And he stretched forth his hand toward his disciples, and said, Behold my mother and my brethren!

For whosoever shall do the will of my Father which is in heaven, the same is my brother, and sister, and mother.

As we meet today to celebrate Christian Family Day, commonly known as Mother's Day, let us take a frank look at the Christian family, what it means, what it can stand for.

The Christian family has a Bible basis. In the Bible the Christian family is a physical, spiritual and emotional unity under God for the enjoyment of the members' perpetuation of the human race, the care and the nurture of children, the happiness of mankind and the transmission of faith.

Each person is respected for what he is, accepted as he is, loved, appreciated and allowed freedom within the limits of self-respect and consideration of others.

The family is more than just the result of a sociological development. From the biblical point of view it is a part of the purpose of God. "God setteth the solitary in families . . ." (Psalms 68:6)

God is revealed in the Bible as a covenant-making and a covenant-keeping God. There is a family covenant through which God makes clear that the parents are expected to pass on their religious heritage to their children. "Train up a child in the way he should go: and when he is old, he will not depart from it." (Proverbs 22:6)

The hallmark of a Christian family is its faith in God.

Children learn primarily from their parents' actions. They soon recognize those things their parents believe to be important.

The writer of Deuteronomy 4:9 said, "Only take heed to thyself, and keep thy soul diligently, lest thou forget the things which thine eyes have seen . . . teach them thy sons, and thy sons' sons."

The home is the first school of religion and the continuing ally of the church, but it takes a long time, in fact a lifetime, to develop Christian persons. Therefore, there must be a continuous effort on the part of all members of the family to be closely related to God, if they are to grow and develop as Christians.

A second mark of the Christian family is love.

Love is the heart of Christian faith and love is the heart of the Christian home.

When the family is truly related to God, the source of love develops a love for one another, sacrificial giving of self and a concern for the welfare of other members of the family.

The love of God is mediated to children through parents who express love.

If a parent mistreats his child, it will be difficult for that child to understand the love of the heavenly Father, since he has not experienced it from his earthly father.

Only as children see real love through their parents can they understand the meaning of the love of God.

> And thou shalt love the Lord thy God with all thy heart, and with all thy soul, and with all thy mind . . . Thou shalt love thy neighbour as thyself. (Mark 12:30–31)

> As the Father hath loved me, so I have loved you . . . This is my commandment, That ye love one another, as I have loved you. (John 15:9, 12)

This is the ideal mark of a Christian family home. A Godlike love at all times for all persons.

A third mark of the Christian family is forgiveness.

Jesus taught us in the Lord's Prayer to "forgive as we are forgiven."

It is practically useless to talk about the forgiveness of God unless it is exemplified by the members of the family.

How can a family become a Christian family?

Again, the teachings in the Bible offer many lessons.

And Adam said, This is now bone of my bones, and flesh of my flesh: she shall be called Woman, because she was taken out of Man.

Therefore shall a man leave his father and his mother, and shall cleave unto his wife: and they shall be one flesh. (Genesis 2:23–24)

And thou shalt teach them diligently unto thy children, and shalt talk of them when thou sittest in thine house, and when thou walkest by the way, and when thou liest down, and when thou risest up. (Deuteronomy 6:7)

Whoso findeth a wife findeth a good thing, and obtaineth favour of the Lord. (Proverbs 18:22)

Train up a child in the way he should go: and when he is old, he will not depart from it. (Proverbs 22:6)

Live joyfully with the wife whom thou lovest all the days of the life of thy vanity, which he hath given thee under the sun, all the days of thy vanity: for that is thy portion in this life, and in thy labour which thou takest under the sun. (Ecclesiastes 9:9)

What therefore God hath joined together, let not man put asunder. (Mark 10:9)

Husbands, love your wives, even as Christ also loved the church, and gave himself for it . . . (Ephesians 5:25)

Let the deacons be the husbands of one wife, ruling their children and their own houses well. (I Timothy 3:12)

I will therefore that the younger women marry, bear children, guide the house, give none occasion to the adversary to speak reproachfully. (I Timothy 5:14)

When I call to remembrance the unfeigned faith that is in thee, which dwelt first in thy grandmother Lois, and thy mother Eunice; and I am persuaded that in thee also. (II Timothy 1:5)

That they may teach the young women to be sober, to love their husbands, to love their children. (Titus 2:4)

Likewise, ye husbands, dwell with them according to knowledge, giving honour unto the wife, as unto the weaker vessel, and as being heirs together of the grace of life; that your prayers be not hindered. (I Peter 3:7)

Prayer is communion with God. The family joins together in homage and reverence toward God as it unites in family prayers. This is more than just a pleasant religious option; it is their lifeline of communication with their heavenly Father, and the foundation of enduring happiness.

May I give you ten tests for a Christian family?

1. Is there love and respect for one another?
2. Is the spirit of cooperation manifest?
3. Does the democratic ideal hold in all matters?
4. Would an unseen visitor be conscious of Christian attitudes?
5. Would an unseen visitor feel that there is reverence in the atmosphere?
6. Do the members have a desire to live together? work together? play together? and read together?
7. Is there real concern for humanitarian causes?
8. Is there a genuine interest in the church?

9. Are the parents in accord?

10. Does the family engage in religious practices that are helpful?

The Christian family:

1. Strives for a growing faith in God.
2. Tries to follow the teachings of Jesus.
3. Seeks to keep in touch with God through prayers.
4. Worships in the church regularly.
5. Grows in the knowledge of the Bible.
6. Shows respect for each personality.
7. Seeks to enrich and deepen its faith in God.
8. Has active growing personal concern for all mankind.

9. Knows that its life and possessions are a gift of God and therefore shares its time, its money and its talents.

10. Finds and radiates joy in daily living through the cementing love of the family's mother.

You Cannot Limit Christ

MARK 12:30

"And thou shalt love the Lord thy God with all thy heart, and with all thy soul, and with all thy mind, and with all thy strength: this is the first commandment."

We live in a time when cheap substitutes may be bought at any price on any bargain counter.

This is true of vital religion.

But I must warn you:

1. If your religious faith is going to mean anything to you, it must mean everything to you.

2. If you try to limit religion to a part of your life, you will lose it throughout the whole of your life.

3. You do not get a vital religious faith as you collect antiques—piece by piece. It is a living unit. You either get all at once or you do not get it at all. To be sure, it may be as immature as an embryo when you get it and it is in need of careful nurture before it achieves its full powers. Even an embryo is a living unit.

4. You cannot buy vital religious faith on time. You either lay everything you have on the line or you waste what you do put there.

5. You cannot win a vital religious faith by means of a calculating and cautious approach; you fall in love without reservation or you lose it altogether.

6. Only in a limited sense do you get out of religion what you put into it. In fact, you must put everything into it in order to get anything out of it. If you put anything less than everything you get nothing but shame of hypocrisy.

For years vital religion has had a rough time of it. But at last we are coming to that part of our religious development where the world and our souls do agree in saying: "You must come to terms with God! It is His way or your way! There is no compromise! All or none."

If we continue the way we are going, we will be writing our obituary in terms of evasions rather than affirmations, compromises rather than convictions.

All of this is simply the logical conclusion to the teachings of Jesus. The only way to alter this is to remove Jesus as the historic revelation of God.

Jesus stated this very exactly in two commandments: (1) love God completely; (2) love your neighbor completely.

You cannot fit Christ into any pattern.

The Jews tried to do this.

It is understandable that they wanted Jesus to be their Messiah. They wanted to say, "You cannot enter Christ's faith except through the door of Judaism." It was finally abandoned because a good Jew named Paul was overwhelmed and realized that in Jesus there "is neither Jew nor Greek . . . bond nor free . . . male nor female, for ye are all one in Christ Jesus." (Galatians 3:28)

Some of us want to regard Him simply as our personal Savior; to limit Him to our private problems; to keep His searching ethical insight from lighting up the dark corners of our society. On the other hand, there are others who want to regard Him solely as a leader in social reform.

But you cannot limit Jesus.

There is an indivisible unity between the personal and social meanings of religion. Try to separate them and both of them will die. The love of God and the love of man are two sides of the same coin, which is Jesus. They are like the opposite ends of the same tunnel. Whichever end you enter, you will always come out the other.

You cannot limit Christ without losing Him.

We have tried to limit Him with creeds. Peter formed the first creed when he said, "thou art that Christ, the Son of the living God." (John 6:69) Under the Roman persecution, "Jesus is Lord." Later, there was the Apostles' Creed. No creed has been able to satisfy all Christians.

The danger of creeds is that creeds place themselves above Christ. But Christ is bigger than all creeds. The purpose of a creed must be to lead men to Christ, not to the creed.

Christ limited to creeds is Christ betrayed by creeds.

E. Stanley Jones said: "When the world is at its worst the Christian must be at his best."

Our task today is:

To keep our banners flying on great issues.

To see that the Christian word is spoken with force, persuasiveness and effectiveness.

To see that wherever conflicts are threatening to break up the family of God, the Word is spoken.

To see that the Christian witness is borne to the utmost parts of the earth.

To see that wherever men grope in darkness, they are pointed toward the light.

To see that wherever men are crippled by despair, they are pointed toward hope and encouragement.

Christ unlimited is Christ fulfilled.

He is the Lord of Life.

The Temptation of Modernity

MATTHEW 4:1–10

And when the tempter came to him, he said, If thou be the Son of God, command that these stones be made bread.

But he answered and said, It is written, Man shall not live by bread alone, but by every word that proceedeth out of the mouth of God.

Then the devil taketh him up into the holy city, and setteth him on a pinnacle of the temple,

And saith unto him, If thou be the Son of God, cast thyself down: for it is written, He shall give his angels charge concerning thee: and in their hands they shall bear thee up, lest at any time thou dash thy foot against a stone.

Jesus said unto him, It is written again, Thou shalt not tempt the Lord thy God.

Again, the devil taketh him up into an exceeding high mountain, and sheweth him all the kingdoms of the world, and the glory of them;

And saith unto him, All these things will I give thee, if thou wilt fall down and worship me.

Then saith Jesus unto him, Get thee hence, Satan: for it is written, Thou shalt worship the Lord thy God, and him only shalt thou serve.

We have produced a world of contented bodies and discontented minds.

It has been the aim of the welfare state in America, of socialism in England, of Marxism behind the Iron Curtain.

We have changed the Twenty-third Psalm to read, "The state is my shepherd, I shall not want."

Finally, the only leadership that we respect and search for in today's world is political leadership, for we fail to realize that political leadership is one of expediency and compromise.

So we come face to face today with the same temptations that Jesus met: materialism, paternalism and power.

Let us now examine these temptations of Jesus' day and of today. For as Browning said in his *Aristophanes' Apology,* "When the fight begins with himself, a man's worth something."

The temptation story as recorded in the fourth chapter of Matthew, the first ten verses, is found also in Luke but not in Mark.

It would seem appropriate that Jesus should have His vocation tested.

His ministry should begin with a struggle between God's kingdom and Satan's kingdom. Make no mistake about it, the three temptations continually recurred in the course of His ministry: working miracles for the satisfaction of immediate needs, giving convincing signs, and exercising political power.

There is no contradiction in the beginning verse, "Then

was Jesus led up of the spirit . . . to be tempted of the devil."

The Spirit must lead us into searching our hearts, and it is during this trying period that the forces of evil have their greatest opportunity.

I want you to note the Old Testament doctrine of the devil. He is a personal devil. And let us admit that the temptations that beset us today are personal persuasions.

Men and steel are alike uncertain until they are tested. We should seek the power to resist not just during the crisis but beforehand.

I love the story about Dwight Moody during a crisis; he wouldn't pray while others did, and when they upbraided him he said, "Brethren, I'm all prayed up."

(The first temptation was one of hunger. The physical needs of man are always a factor. Roman taxes ground down the poor, and the pathetic struggle of His fellow Jews for life touched the heart of Jesus.)

Surely it is righteous and merciful to revolt in justice. But it leaves unanswered the profound question: From what motive, by what power, and toward what end?

Jesus did not center His mission on an economic crusade. He did not forsake the Cross for a bakeshop. Man does live by bread, but not by bread alone.

I like the story I heard in Transjordan of a hungry Arab who suddenly finds a treasure in the midst of the desert and cries, "Alas, it is only diamonds!"

Man in his deepest hunger cries, "Alas, it is only bread!" Carlisle in his great *Sartor Resartus,* Book II in the ninth chapter, says "Not all the finance ministers, upholsterers, and confectioners of Europe in joint stock company, could make one shoe-black happy for more than a couple of hours."

The second temptation—"If thou be the Son of God, cast thyself down"—implies tremendous personal and social impact. Jesus might be able to shake a shallow generation out of its indifference, its unbelief.

Noble spirits are always tempted to be sensational for the sake of God. God is not proved by sleight of hand. The soul has its own testimony, and God is His own interpreter. Man has no right to force God's hand. How often we try!

The third temptation was the appeal to political leadership, humbled in the midst of mightier powers. At that very moment the Romans had a garrison in every town, crushing with taxes and ruthlessly oppressing the people.

The great thing here was the price that would have to be paid: "if thou wilt fall down and worship me."

And what are the temptations of today? Materialism, paternalism and power.

Materialism. Discontented minds in the midst of contented bodies. There is in the warp and woof of man a fatal weakness for physical things. Most of us feel that man can live by bread alone. This has been one of the great strongholds of the Marxist crusade. Unfortunately, they have been right a great deal of the time. Here in America we think that wages, subsidies, pensions, are enough to make America a paradise. But any system that tends to put our churches where moths corrupt, thieves break through and steal, is diabolically dangerous.

We are not only producing discontented minds in the midst of contented bodies, but we are producing damned souls.

Man must live by the word of God. God can sustain life without bread.

Paternalism. There is a feeling, not only in the welfare state, that the state is our shepherd, we shall not want; this false feeling prevails among Christians too—God is good, this is His world, therefore no matter what I do He will take care of me.

These are devilish lies.

God did not intend to create, and did not create, a world

unconditionally safe and secure. There is sorrow, there is suffering.

God gives us reason and conscience that we may discern
and obey the laws of the Divine Order.

We cannot blindly test God and cast ourselves from a
pinnacle. The truth of it is it takes the best of our initiative,
muscles, skills, moral judgment, in order to survive.

God's wonderful world is hopelessly hostile to faith
without works.

God demands intelligent and diligent work, because God
wants to make men of us.

He did not beget the human race so that men could get a
little fun out of life.

He did not put His Son on a cross so that we could have
a picnic.

He is after something that He risked death to get.

He wants strong men.

He wants the kind of character that can withstand the
acids of time, the kind of spirit that is immortal because it has
become indestructible.

He wants men stable and sturdy, holy with moral hero-
ism.

The Fatherhood of God is anything but paternalistic. I
know that we want equality, but I warn you that freedom is
always more important. Though we are searching for security, I
want you to know that responsibility and initiative are greater.

Yes, God cares for us, but He cares for us in order that
we may have the power to care for others. And no one is caring
for others who squanders himself.

Power. There is in the heart of every human being the
temptation to be God. Power tends to corrupt, and absolute
power, absolutely. Put a policeman on the corner, and watch
what happens to him.

What would happen to a fire department that didn't have a district attorney?

What would happen to a church that didn't have an official board over its minister?

What would happen to both that didn't have a free church?

This is the bone of our leadership today—expediency and compromise. The devil was getting pretty close to Jesus with his temptation and he is pretty close to us. We are power-drunk.

And we are paying the price—"fall down and worship me."

I rise today to say, "Thou shalt worship the Lord thy God, and Him only shalt thou serve."

These words may not be pleasant words, or cheerful words, or popular words. The words that I speak are probably salt poured upon the sores of modern men, but I must speak them:

Man cannot live by bread.

Freedom is more important than security.

The Lord thy God is my God, He is the only one who deserves absolute power.

"Holy, holy, holy, Lord God Almighty." The only safeguard against the sovereign power of God is love. God loves us all.

My plea this morning is to keep God in His place, and His place is that of absolute sovereign.

If we will keep God in His place in all of our affairs, we will have a good world. People who do not worship God eventually cease to be human.

But when we do worship Him and serve Him—listen to the magnificent conclusion of this story—"Then the devil leaveth him."

We can resist the temptation of materialism, the temptation of paternalism, the temptation of power. "Then the devil leaveth him."

That should be enough, but we get a bonus: ". . . behold, angels came and ministered unto him."

Seek ye first the Kingdom of God, and all else shall be added unto you.

A Sermon for a Crisis

DECEMBER 3, 1950

ROMANS 13:12

The night is far spent, the day is at hand: let us therefore cast off the works of darkness, and let us put on the armour of light.

We have just come through one of the most terrifying weeks of modern times.

Our hearts were breathless during that awful day of the past week as we waited to know whether we would carry out our threat to use the atom bomb.

We know that we do not monopolize this bomb, and our use of it would cause it to be used immediately against us.

While it is true that our stockpile is in the hundreds, yet our Intelligence informs us that the bombs of our enemy number between fifteen and twenty-five.

When we think of the damage that was done on Hiroshima by one bomb and carry our thoughts further, imagining the "fifteen to twenty-five" being dropped on fifteen to twenty-five American cities, we become appalled at the prospect.

It therefore taxes the faith and the optimism of the preacher to come this morning to tell you the good news of the tidings of the gospel, and yet I must, for if the gospel of Jesus Christ is only for the sunshine, then it is worthless.

But I do come as a minister of the gospel this morning, because it is my opinion that our world has just about reached the place where an upturn must begin.

In the language of Paul writing to his friends at Rome: "The night is far spent, the day is at hand: let us therefore cast off the works of darkness, and let us put on the armour of light."

The night is far spent

I think civilization has just about descended to the lowest point possible without virtual annihilation. Internationally, mankind is being forced to turn to the United Nations.

Barely six months ago, many of my colleagues in the House of Representatives frequently would take the floor and ridicule the United Nations.

We placed our hope in the Marshall Plan then, but we have found out that no one nation, despite its superior wealth and know-how, can buy its way to friendship. The sole remaining political hope of mankind is the United Nations.

In the economic world, our wages are increasing but, due to poor distribution, we have a static standard of life. Just last week the index of the cost of living was the highest it has ever been in the history of our nation.

Racism cannot be any worse than it is.

In Toronto, Canada, in one of the wealthiest neighborhoods, they have set up separate classrooms for Jews—and we thought Hitler was dead.

In the field of education, we are spending more money per child and gleaning less common sense per skull.

Protestantism has started the upturn. During the very day we were waiting for news of the dropping of an atom bomb on our enemy, 32 million Protestants gathered together in Cleveland, Ohio, in the greatest demonstration of Protestant faith since the beginning of the Reformation.

> Be strong! It matters not how deep entrenched the wrong. How hard the battle goes, the [night] how long! Faint not, fight on! Tomorrow comes the song. Be strong!

The day is at hand

It is as futile for anyone to try to hold back tomorrow's dawn as it is for any individual or power or combination of powers to try to hold back the day which is at hand. The challenges are clear for our world: "unite or die"; for our political system: "unity or anarchy"; for our economic system: "distribution or collapse"; for our social life: "live as brothers or die as rats"; for our educational institutions: "character or ignorance"; and for our great worldwide church: "organized atheism or One Lord, One Faith, One Baptism."

The secret message of Paul's letter to his friends at Rome, after he had sketched the broad introduction of "the night is far spent and the day is at hand," was unity. For he said, "Let us therefore . . ." In other words, the inability of Christian people to cast off the works of darkness in Paul's day was due to the same cause as in our day: a lack of corporate cooperative unity.

Let us cast off the works of darkness

We think we are living in a Christian nation and in a Christian world, but we have never been so wrong. Religion, Christianity, the organized church is definitely secondary in the life of America and in the life of church people. Modern secularism has supplemented the church.

This supplementation of the church in a nation which is called a Christian nation is due to the inertia of the people. "Let us therefore cast off the works of darkness."

The inertia of Paul's day was due to Phariseeism. The inertia of today is due to twentieth-century Phariseeism—Phariseeism in the exaltation of self over other men, thanking God that we are better than others. This is due in some cases to chronic laziness and ignorance.

We rationalize our behavior by our self-exalted opinion. But I am not concerned with that group so much; I am concerned with the group that Jesus came preaching to—the group who were good members of the synagogue but, because of their self-appointed and self-sustained position, stood in the way of the power of organized religion casting off the works of darkness.

Let me trace the historical developments. For centuries the Prophets had proclaimed against the Phariseeism of class; for centuries they had condemned the powers of darkness and foretold the coming of a great life. This type of prophecy reached its highest insight when Isaiah proclaimed:

> Therefore is judgment far from us, neither doth justice overtake us: we wait for light, but behold obscurity; for brightness, but we walk in darkness.
>
> We grope for the wall like the blind, and we grope as if we had no eyes: we stumble at noon day as in the night; we are in desolate places as dead men.
>
> We roar all like bears, and mourn sore like doves: we look for judgment, but there is none; for salvation, but it is far off from us.
>
> For our transgressions are multiplied before thee, and our sins testify against us: for our transgressions are with us; and as for our iniquities, we know them;
>
> In transgressing and lying against the Lord, and departing away from our God, speaking oppression and revolt, conceiving and uttering from the heart words of falsehood.
>
> And judgment is turned away backward, and justice standeth afar off: for truth is fallen in the street, and equity cannot enter.
>
> Yea, truth faileth; and he that departeth from evil maketh himself a prey: and the Lord saw it, and it displeased him that there was no judgment.
>
> And he saw that there was no man, and wondered that there was no intercessor: therefore his arm brought salvation unto him; and his righteousness, it sustained him.
>
> For he put on righteousness as a breastplate, and an helmet of salvation upon his head; and he put on the garments of vengeance for clothing, and was clad with zeal as a cloke.
>
> According to their deeds, accordingly he will repay, fury to his adversaries, recompense to his enemies; to the islands he will repay recompense.

So shall they fear the name of the Lord from the west, and his glory from the rising of the sun. When the enemy shall come in like a flood, the Spirit of the Lord shall lift up a standard against him.

And the Redeemer shall come to Zion, and unto them that turn from transgression in Jacob, saith the Lord. . . .

Arise, shine; for thy light is come, and the glory of the Lord is risen upon thee.

For behold, the darkness shall cover the earth, and gross darkness the people: but the Lord shall arise upon thee, and his glory shall be seen upon thee. (Isaiah 59:9–20; 60:1–2)

Jesus, the light for a world of darkness

After a breathless world had waited for centuries, this light did appear. John in his life of Jesus depicts the birth of Jesus in accordance with the prophecy of Isaiah:

That which was from the beginning, which we have heard, which we have seen with our eyes, which we have looked upon, and our hands have handled, of the Word of life;

(For the life was manifested, and we have seen it, and bear witness, and shew unto you that eternal life, which was with the Father, and was manifested unto us;)

That which we have seen and heard declare we unto you, that ye also may have fellowship with us: and truly our fellowship is with the Father, and with his Son Jesus Christ.

And these things write we unto you, that your joy may be full.

This then is the message which we have heard of him, and declare unto you, that God is light, and in him is no darkness at all. (I John 1:1–5)

This light came preaching against the Pharisees of his day. So much so, that: "The people which sat in darkness saw great light . . ." (Matthew 4:16)

But the Pharisees did their best to get rid of this rude disturber of their status quo, this man who would awaken the people from their inertia. And finally through trickery they had his body delivered into their hands. Listen to Luke's account of the seizure of Jesus:

> When I was daily with you in the temple, ye stretched forth no hands against me: but this is your hour, and the power of darkness.
> Then took they him, and led him, and brought him into the high priest's house . . . (Luke 22:53–54)
> And he said unto them, These are the words which I spake unto you, while I was yet with you, that all things must be fulfilled, which were written in the law of Moses, and in the prophets, and in the psalms, concerning me. (Luke 24:44)

But even in the midst of darkness the light did shine and the darkness comprehended it not and the light of the world hung there on the tree.

He looked to his side, where the Pharisees had crucified a thief, and said, "Today shalt thou be with me in paradise."

He hung there bleeding and dying above the men who had driven the nails in his hands and had thrust the spear in his side and soaked the sponge with vinegar when he cried out: "I thirst," and he said, "Father, forgive them; for they know not what they do," and he gave up the ghost.

And darkness covered the earth—catch the symbolism.

On the morning of the third day, as it began to dawn, the disciples came to an empty tomb. They found there a shining angel, who told them, "He is not here: for he is risen!" Then, as they were walking along the road, they met Him and He said:

> All power is given unto me in heaven and in earth.
> Go ye therefore, and teach all nations, baptizing them in the name of the Father, and of the Son, and of the Holy Ghost:
> Teaching them to observe all things whatsoever I have

commanded you: and, lo, I am with you alway, even unto
the end of the world. (Mark 28:18–20)

With this great tradition, with this great heritage, let us
cast off our inertia, let us cast off our modern Phariseeism, let us
purge from our midst these self-opinionated, self-exalted Pharisees of the church—even those of this church, the Abyssinian
Church, who think they are better than other men. Whether in
this pulpit or out, I intend to preach and to fight actively against
any form of Phariseeism regardless of where it may stem from.

Let us—that means you and me together—let us heed
the advice of Paul:

> Finally, my brethren, be strong in the Lord, and in the
> power of his might.
> Put on the whole armour of God, that ye may be able to
> stand against the wiles of the devil.
> For we wrestle not against flesh and blood, but against
> principalities, against powers, against the rulers of the dark-
> ness of this world, against spiritual wickedness in high
> places.
> Wherefore take unto you the whole armour of God, that
> ye may be able to withstand in the evil day, and having
> done all, to stand.
> Stand therefore, having your loins girt about with truth,
> and having on the breastplate of righteousness;
> And your feet shod with the preparation of the gospel of
> peace;
> Above all, taking the shield of faith, wherewith ye shall
> be able to quench all the fiery darts of the wicked.
> And take the helmet of salvation, and the sword of the
> Spirit, which is the word of God . . . (Ephesians 6:10–17)

The Prayer

JUNE 17, 1962

MATTHEW 21:22

And all things, whatsover ye shall ask in prayer, believing, ye shall receive.

Almighty God, Thou who hast, through Jesus Christ, provided for all our needs, and sent an invitation to all peoples to the ends of the earth:

Hast thou not said, "If any man thirst, let him come unto me, and drink." (John 7:37) "Blessed are they which do hunger and thirst after righteousness: for they shall be filled." (Matthew 5:6)

We come to thee with an abundance of our wants. We are overwhelmed by our needs.

Away from thee there is no water to satisfy our thirst, and no bread to give us strength.

Mercifully grant us the restoring fellowship of thy grace, strengthening us with thy love, help us to pray: "ask and believe." Help us to knock in confidence, to seek assurance.

THE MEDITATION

Moreover thou shalt say unto them, Thus saith the Lord; Shall they fall, and not arise? shall he turn away, and not return? . . .

Yea, the stork in the heaven knoweth her appointed times; and the turtle and the crane and the swallow observe the time of their coming; but my people know not the judgment of the Lord. (Jeremiah 8:4, 7)

God-created instincts are behind all animal life.

God-created instincts prompt our souls to return to God:

First, we came from God.

"So God created man in his own image, in the image of God created he him; male and female created he them." (Genesis 1:27)

"And the Lord God formed man of the dust of the ground, and breathed into his nostrils the breath of life; and man became a living soul." (Genesis 2:7)

Second, our humanness has separated us from Him.

> But the angel said unto him, Fear not, Zacharias: for thy prayer is heard; and thy wife Elisabeth shall bear thee a son, and thou shalt call his name John.
>
> And thou shalt have joy and gladness; and many shall rejoice at his birth.
>
> For he shall be great in the sight of the Lord, and shall drink neither wine nor strong drink; and he shall be filled with the Holy Ghost, even from his mother's womb.
>
> And many of the children of Israel shall he turn to the Lord their God.
>
> And he shall go before him in the spirit and power of Elias, to turn the hearts of the fathers to the children, and the disobedient to the wisdom of the just; to make ready a people prepared for the Lord.
>
> And Zacharias said unto the angel, Whereby shall I know this? for I am an old man, and my wife well stricken in years.
>
> And the angel answering said unto him, I am Gabriel, that stand in the presence of God; and am sent to speak unto thee, and to shew thee these glad tidings.
>
> And, behold, thou shalt be dumb, and not able to speak, until the day that these things shall be performed, because thou believest not my words, which shall be fulfilled in their season. (Luke 1:13–20)

Third, the deepest intuition of the soul is to return to Him.

Saint Augustine: "We came from God, and we are restless until we rest in Him."

Fourth, apart from God we are never satisfied.

Fifth, Jesus Christ lived the life of fellowship with God and was satisfied.

> I and my Father are one. (John 10:30)
> . . . into thy hands I commend my spirit . . . (Luke 23:46)

And when we pray, what shall we pray for?

A love that can never be fathomed.
A life that never dies.
A righteousness that never is tarnished.
A rest that is never disturbed.
A joy that is never diminished.
A hope that is never disappointed.
A glory that is never clouded.
A light that is never darkened.
A happiness that is never interrupted.
A strength that is never enfeebled.
A beauty that is never scarred.

> Praying always with all prayer and supplication in the Spirit, and watching thereunto with all perseverance and supplication for all saints;
> And for me, that utterance may be given unto me, that I may open my mouth boldly, to make known the mystery of the gospel . . . (Ephesians 6:18–19)

Brotherhood and Freedom

I JOHN 2:9–11

He that saith he is in the light, and hateth his brother, is in darkness even until now.

He that loveth his brother abideth in the light, and there is none occasion of stumbling in him.

But he that hateth his brother is in darkness, and walketh in darkness, and knoweth not whither he goeth, because that darkness hath blinded his eyes.

Happily we are gathered again to review the facts of Negro life in America as Carter G. Woodson some thirty years ago first directed.

The members of the Abyssinian Baptist Church are to be commended for combining the one hundred fiftieth anniversary of this great church with the total struggle of the Negro in America.

We have appropriately met together to celebrate both Negro History Week and Brotherhood Month.

For what kind of country would this nation have been without the foundation provided by the Christian church?

What would have been the history of the black man in America without the leadership of Abraham Lincoln and the fight of that courageous abolitionist Frederick Douglass?

There is little doubt that an America without the spirit of the above three would not be what it is today.

John Hope Franklin in his work *From Slavery to Freedom* notes that Negro History Week has been celebrated "as a period in which the contribution of the Negro to the development of civilization would be sufficiently emphasized to impress Negroes as well as whites."

But this year of 1959, characterized by wars and rumors of wars, challenges Negroes to add a new ingredient to this annual Negro celebration.

Grave concern must be expressed for the future of this

civilization we helped to develop. It is not so important to impress ourselves and others that we had a hand in building this civilization, as it is that we lend a hand in saving this civilization.

Today we live in a different world, where we cooperate as brothers or we perish as enemies—a world less than twenty-four hours large; a world in which hydrogen bombs, superfortresses, nuclear-propelled jets and guided missiles exist at man's disposal.

Time no longer permits the foolish acting out of white supremacy as though it were ordained by God. Nor can this civilization which we Negroes willingly or unwillingly helped to develop guarantee any longer its right to dominate others.

There is not even time left for living and learning in such a world. Rather, we are commanded to learn to live and learn that quickly if we are planning to survive this nuclear age.

Death was hovering over President Roosevelt as he composed a Jefferson Day speech which he never lived to deliver:

> Today we are faced with the preeminent fact that if civilization is to survive, we must cultivate the science of human relationships, the ability of all peoples to live together in the same world at peace. For today science has brought the different quarters of the globe so close together that is is impossible to isolate them one from another.

Modern civilization is unquestionably at the crossroads, with one road leading to victory and another to disaster. While we are forced to accept the fact that the nuclear age is here to stay, we must inquire if we are.

One alternative to universal annihilation is for American Negroes to speak out from the richness of their heritage more loudly this whole year than we have since the inauguration of Negro History Week.

In order to make our voices heard and our spirits of love meaningful to the lasting good of mankind, there is a critical need for a complete unraveling of Negro history to put our cultural virtues to immediate productive services.

Though there is enormous ill will, greed, cruelty and exploitation in this world, there is an overwhelming residue of good yet, if we but seek and acknowledge it.

If the Negro forgets where he came from, if he discards the spirit that propelled him to his present position, if he loses faith (for there are those who mock and deny him), then American rot and dissolution will be under way.

The presence of the Afro-American and the Almighty Dollar are twin forces which together have played major roles in shaping the material and spiritual well-being of America from its beginning until today.

Today it is fitting and proper that the congregation of the Abyssinian Baptist Church, whose history predates the emancipation, pay homage to the spirit that endowed us with faith.

This church stands as a living reminder—a memorial—to those who dared defy the corrupters of Christianity.

Early Negro churches were born in a period when it was religiously established by the white world that the Negro was ordained to be "a servant of servants unto his brethren."

Negro churches afforded the black man protection when he was cut off from all other participation in the political life of the country and from all other religious institutions of the community.

When "buying cheap and selling dear" was established as an economic principle and when promoting the slave trade and supporting the institution of slavery was an acknowledged moral responsibility and an expression of the highest ethical principles, Negro Christian leaders kept the Brotherhood of Man alive.

While white churches languished in racist degradation and betrayed the Master, Negro churches both underground and above ground were fulfilling the prophetic mission to "bless them that curse you, do good to them that hate you, and pray for them which despitefully use you, and persecute you."

Today, the Negro missionary of Jesus Christ finds in the black world ready acceptance of rising expectations. Unlike its white contemporaries, the Negro church never supported slavery and colonialism in violation of the human spirit.

Your church, the Abyssinian Baptist, and many others like it kept the faith when an unchristian blackout covered this land.

From its inception, the Negro church has waged a ceaseless battle against the Hebrew-Christian doctrine of the inequality of man, believing instead that such a covenant ran counter to the plan of redemption.

Our church could never support a dogma which eliminated all colored people from the redeeming influence of Jesus Christ.

When the Master saw His many black children wronged, when He viewed the denial of His blessings to His flock, He must have addressed the founders of the Negro church thus: "upon this rock I will build my church; and the gates of hell shall not prevail against it . . . I will give unto thee the keys of the kingdom of heaven . . ." (Matthew 16:18–19)

So the Savior placed hope in the Negro even while the Bishop of London was placing his stamp of approval upon the righteousness of slavery.

The desire to be free and to liberate one's brother became, in contrast to the philosophy of white churches, a permanent foundation of the Negro church, which carries over into the present day.

While the white Christian majority ignored the abominable mistreatment of Negroes after the Emancipation, Negro churches became the rallying points against segregation and its abuses.

So great was the suffering in the latter nineteenth century

that Frederick Douglass was prompted to inquire in 1889 whether "American justice, American liberty, American civilization, American law, American Christianity can be made to include and protect alike and forever all American citizens in the rights which have been guaranteed them by the organic and fundamental laws of the land."

Abraham Lincoln was so moved by the corruption of Christianity through man-made creeds and dogmas which enslaved humanity that he cried out:

> If the church would ask simply for assent to the Savior's statement of the substance of the law: "Thou shalt love the Lord thy God, with all thy heart and with all thy soul and with all thy mind and thy neighbor as thyself," that church I would gladly join with.

Now we have suddenly reached the point in American history, in Western civilization, in the whole wide world, where laws and religious ideals apply equally and alike to all and everyone, or they will apply to none.

Here in America today the Christian church is split, the Administration is fighting to win a return trip to the White House, the Supreme Court is struggling to maintain its traditional role, Congressmen are disputing among themselves, public schools are shut down tight, the white community is set one against the other as surely as they were in the nineteenth century over what to do about us.

Add to this the threat that the world may go up in flames at any time.

Then we realize how serious has been the betrayal of Christ and how important it is that in memorializing our historical relationship to this country we rededicate our lives to Christ in all we do.

For the present racial conflicts, class contradictions and moral dilemmas have broken this country and all those in it from their democratic ideals, from our once secure mooring, setting this nation hopelessly adrift on a turbulent sea, heading toward hopeless disaster.

What can the Negro do?

What prospects are there for Negroes to turn the tide in this turmoil of human progress and social evolution? Nagasaki and Hiroshima having bequeathed "We ain't gonna study war no more," the Negro church must undertake the saving of mankind.

So we are gathered in humility today to seek the revelation of a vision, and a means through which we can work that vision into the constructive human relationship of brotherhood, the only sure foundation for a world of tomorrow, the only way we can postpone the Judgment Day.

Until the Negro in America so applies his knowledge to the major national and international issues rather than attacking for the sake of attack, we shall never alter our position as "servants of our brethren" nor assist in saving this world from ultimate disaster.

We, all of us, here in the United States want peace, yes, but we want power and privilege and economic advantage both here and abroad—the things that lead to racial conflicts and war.

We want racial harmony and integration into American life but we want to continue to enjoy the fruits of selfish existence, which make a democratic life impossible.

In a world where personal comforts at the expense of others has become an end, a way of life, we Americans, blacks and whites, are unwilling to submit to the alteration in our behavior this shrinking globe demands.

We are worshiping the gods of the gadgets instead of the God who directs the manpower behind these machines that are betraying Him.

In desperation the white man is already being forced to

analyze old dogmas of success, once accepted without question.

His proofs of a super-nation and super-peoples, as evidenced by improved standards of living, the highest wages ever paid in history, the greatest speed and the ability to maintain a continuous state of sustained excitement, are no longer satisfying. Old feelings for a trip to Paradise are slowly fading away.

And it appears that this civilization and all that is in it is heading for a nose dive. Where it will come to rest no one knows.

In the present climate our souls cannot catch up with our bodies and we wonder if our souls have not gone unattended while we have been busy gratifying our physical desires.

Is there any wonder, moreover, that people do not like us and that our spirits have deserted us in this culture where accomplishments and worth and human values are measured by money standards and expressed in financial terms? Where warfed ethical principles flowing therefrom have underwritten our institutions, dictated our policies and guided our every act, from marriage to prayer?

"If a man say, I love God, and hateth his brother, he is a liar: for he that loveth not his brother whom he hath seen, how can he love God whom he hath not seen?" (I John 4:20)

The high and mighty must condition and readjust their every deed and thought to this nuclear age and admit that concepts of racial inferiority, false material standards, antisocial ideas and class hatred can be no more in this world where we live together or die.

What can the Negro do to develop this civilization anew?

Unless the American blacks can supply something that the sweep of the white man's civilization has omitted, there can be no future world, certainly no better world.

This the Negro cannot supply until he refuses to drink any more of the poisons of this civilization.

If history is allowed to repeat itself, then this civilization, unlike its forerunners, will work the end of man on this planet.

It has been asserted that "History can be made," and I believe Negroes can do it and must set themselves immediately to the task. As Laurence Binyon wrote:

> Only when we are hurt with all the hurt untold—
> In us the thirst, the hunger, and ours the helpless hand,
> The palsied effort vain, the darkness and the cold—
> Then only then, the spirit knows and understands.
> And finds in every sigh breathed beneath the sun
> The heart that makes us infinitely one. . . .

Although the Negro is among the latecomers to this civilization, no one can look at us and our offspring and conclude we are a vanishing race. Father John Boyle O'Reilly, an Irish Catholic patriot, once wrote:

> No one ever came into the world with so grand an opportunity as the American Negro. He is like new metal dug out of the mine. He stands on the threshold of history with everything to learn and less to unlearn than any civilized man in the world. In the heart of the Negro yet remains traditional African concern for one's fellow man and the matriarchal love and protection of youth. . . .
>
> At worst, the Colored American has only a century of degrading tradition, habit, hostility of his fellow man, delinquency and inferiority to forget or unlearn. His nature has only been injured on the outside by these late circumstances. Inside he is a new man, fresh from nature, with feeling and convictions and cheerful, with faith and determination to live alone with mankind regardless of color.

Stripped of a few temporal absurdities, the Negro is fit and ready to take the leadership to guide the white man from the cliff of disaster and to preserve only the good in America from those who would seek to destroy it.

So the challenge before the Negro is twofold:

First, we must totally liberate every Negro in these United States from those who would enslave him. Desegregation is not enough; that is only the beginning. Where the Negro can move freely he must have the money to pay for the ride.

Though desegregation releases the Negro to sail the sea of democracy and join the tide of freedom, he is currently shipwrecked on the banks of integration.

As Max Lerner stated in his book *America as a Civilization,* "The Negro is the real outsider of American life." It is generally known that the Negro shares little in the industrial, political and commercial prosperity around him.

Last week the daily press reported—and the *Congressional Record* restated the finding—that of 11,520 families in the District of Columbia, the nation's capital, existing on substandard incomes, all but 345 are colored; that there are 45,000 children from such families living here in want.

Moreover, we were informed that of the 48,000 attachments of wages, popularly called garnishments, last year, nine out of ten cases involved Negroes.

The economic blight in Washington prevails in Harlem, in Detroit, in Chicago, wherever Negroes reside.

Churches are still called to take the leadership in desegregated areas to assert themselves on behalf of their flocks and humanity against the economic oppressions which are degrading and destroying the Negro potential just as surely as slavery and social and political segregation did in the past.

Second, armed with the Christian spirit, Negro leaders must be in the front ranks of international relations to apply the imperative of Christian spirit.

For the Holy Bible and the words of Jesus have been falsified in so many different ways to serve a multiplicity of sects, fancies and tyrannical ambitions, that it is for the Negroes, the longest sufferers in America from Christian denial, to fulfill the gospel by adjusting the message of Christ for the preservation of mankind.

For as the Master directed Mark (14:14–15):

> . . . say ye to the goodman of the house, The Master saith, Where is my guestchamber, where I shall eat the passover with my disciples.
> And he will show you a large upper room furnished and prepared: there make ready for us.

Edward Shillito, author of *Nationalism: Man's Other Religion,* expressed a similar concern this way:

> Once again the Lord of the world draws near us and seeks a guest chamber where he can eat with his disciples. But he cannot keep the feast for which the ages have waited till he sits down with all his disciples out of the tribes and tongues; and they cannot know perfectly the glory of that fellowship which in part they know, till there are none missing out of the peoples of the earth. But there is no room for us all. . . . There shall yet come a time when in the fellowship of the Savior of the world the children of men shall sit down in the large upper room. And there can be no greater calling than to believe in that day and to give all powers of heart and mind to prepare for it.

Stop Blaming
Everybody Else

NOVEMBER 29, 1959

EXODUS 32:21–23

And Moses said unto Aaron, What did this people unto thee, that thou hast brought so great a sin upon them?

And Aaron said, Let not the anger of my lord wax hot: thou knowest the people, that they are set on mischief.

For they said unto me, Make us gods, which shall go before us: for as for this Moses, the man that brought us up out of the land of Egypt, we wot not what is become of him.

We are living, today, in the midst of the Big Lie.

The leader of this new cult of deceit is Senator Joseph McCarthy. He has perjured himself countless times.

The greatest perjury was this past week on television, when he said that President Truman's definition of McCarthyism was "word for word, line for line, comma for comma, taken from the *Daily Worker*." Reporters, when questioning his aide about this statement, asked him "what edition and what page of the *Daily Worker*."

McCarthy's aide stated that the Senator did not quite tell the truth, there was no edition or page of the *Daily Worker* that printed the definition that President Truman used.

McCarthy has never admitted any of the lies that he has stated. Despite all of this perjury, he has set himself up as the one single standard upon which the future of the United States of America must depend.

An even greater tragedy is the full and unequivocal stamp of approval placed upon McCarthy by his church in Amsterdam, The Netherlands, when just a couple of weeks ago Cardinal Spellman unequivocally praised the Senator.

McCarthyism, the Big Lie, is our responsibility because it is our fault. It is a reflection of the moral irresponsibility of the church which condones him, the press which praises him, and the large numbers of American people who follow him.

The hour has arrived for the vast majority of American

people who believe in the Protestant heritage of freedom and truth to, first, admit that McCarthyism is our fault and, second, atone for this national disgrace by purging McCarthyism from our national life.

One of the more prevalent sins of people, including religious people, from the beginning of time has been the habit of blaming everybody else for their personal, group or national sins.

So I come today to preach from the subject "Stop Blaming Everybody Else."

While God and Moses were on the mountain talking together and God gave Moses the Ten Commandments, the people of Israel became impatient with Moses' absence. "Up, make us gods," they demanded of Aaron, who made from their golden earrings a golden calf.

And the people said, "These be thy gods, O Israel, which brought thee up out of the land of Egypt." And Aaron built an altar, and said, "Tomorrow is a feast to the Lord."

Then came the feast day, and they ate, drank and played. Then God said to Moses, "Go get thee down . . . thy people . . . have corrupted themselves . . . let me alone that my wrath may wax hot against them, and that I may consume them: and I will make of thee a great nation."

Moses said to God, "Remember Abraham, Isaac, and Israel, thy servants . . ."

"And the Lord repented of the evil which he thought to do unto his people." And Moses, coming down from the mountain, broke the tablets, burned the calf to powder, threw the ashes upon the water and made the people drink it. Then he said to Aaron, "What did these people unto thee, that thou hast brought so great a sin upon them?"

To which Aaron replied, "Let not the anger of my lord wax hot: thou knowest the people, that they are set on mischief.

For they said unto me, Make us gods, which shall go before us . . ."

Remember, *first,* that each one of us accounts for his own deeds. No one can excuse himself because "everybody is doing it."

Second, what you get out of life depends largely on what you put into it. For example, Aaron put into the fire golden earrings and brought out a golden calf.

Third, stop evading your responsibilities!

Fourth, a confession of guilt is much more to one's credit than insincere excuses.

What can happen when you play your part?

Moses played his part: "Oh, this people have sinned a great sin, and have made them gods of gold. Yet now, if thou wilt forgive their sins—; and if not, blot me, I pray thee, out of thy book which thou hast written."

But God refused to forgive them; He flatly refused to go with them anymore: ". . . I will send an angel before thee . . . for I will not go up in the midst of thee; for thou art a stiffnecked people . . ."

Moses stood his ground and pleaded for the people. They talked together "face to face, as a man speaketh unto his friend." And Moses beseeched, ". . . if I have found grace in thy sight, shew me now thy way, that I may know thee . . . and consider that this nation is thy people."

And God relented. "I will do this thing also that thou hast spoken: for thou hast found grace in my sight, and I know thee by name."

What were the results?

First, new tablets for the testimony of God.

Second, a new concept of God: "The Lord, the Lord

God, merciful and gracious, long-suffering, and abundant in goodness and truth, Keeping mercy for thousands, forgiving iniquity and transgression and sins . . ."

. . . *Third,* a new covenant. "Behold, I make a covenant: before all thy people I will do marvels, such as have not been done in all the earth, nor in any nation: and all the people among which thou art shall see the work of the Lord: for it is a terrible thing that I will do with thee."

Fourth, a new Moses. "And it came to pass, when Moses came down from Mount Sinai . . . the skin of his face shone while he talked . . . And when Aaron and all the children of Israel saw Moses, behold, the skin of his face shone; and they were afraid to come nigh him." (Exodus, Chapters 32–34)

The Men of Babel
versus
the Men of Bethlehem

GENESIS 11:4

And they said, Go to, let us build us a city and a tower, whose top may reach unto heaven . . .

REVELATION 3:20

Behold, I stand at the door, and knock: if any man hear my voice, and open the door, I will come in to him, and will sup with him, and he with me.

The other day, Nasser and Khrushchev pushed the button to bring to pass the great reservoir of Aswan. Priceless memorials of the past will be inundated and obliterated, but Egypt's arable land will be increased one-third. The forces of hydroelectric power will be made available.

All this reminds me of another great memorial of the past which long ago vanished from the scene—the Tower of Babel.

The Tower of Babel was built by descendants of Noah.

They lived a prosperous existence on the fruitful plains on which early civilization was cradled between the Tigris and the Euphrates rivers.

In the years to come the great city of Babylon would rise to dominate the empire to which the city would give its name—the Babylonian Empire.

The men of Babel were men of enterprise, initiative, power, confidence, and also men of religion. They pooled their resources in a startling and unique adventure.

In order to reach God, they set about building a tower which would relate earth with heaven.

They undertook their enterprise with the utmost confidence and cooperation, but they never completed it. Instead, confusion, dissent, disagreement and dismay settled upon them.

Their partially completed tower is figuratively left standing as a monument to the failure of man to find God through his own resources, his own strength, guided only by his own wisdom.

But unfortunately, as is true of many of the great stories of the Old and New Testaments, the years have come and gone and the experiences have been forgotten.

Today the message falls on deaf ears; its wisdom goes unheeded.

But I believe it is well worth remembering, well worth considering. Somewhere between the Tower of Babel and the Man of Bethlehem lies the reason for man's pathetic and tragic failure to discover God and to possess the "peace that passeth all understanding."

Today we must discover the weakness and the stupidity of the men of Babel, or we will never be able to find the wisdom of the Man of Bethlehem.

One would suppose that after so many centuries of experience man would be wise in the ways of God; yet it is an amazing fact that the vast majority of Christian people are no better prepared, no better informed, no wiser than the general run of people two thousand years ago.

The reason why there has been so little progress in the field of Christianity is due to man's emphasis upon the externals of religion—the Tower of Babel—rather than upon the internal —the Man of Bethlehem.

Modern man shares the conviction of the men of Babel that God is a distant person far removed from the toil and tribulations of earth. He resides in some place afar, isolated and insulated.

And so, with this faulty reasoning, the men of Babel decided to storm the presence of God, to take the initiative. And many of us today have the same reaction.

We do not believe that God is concerned.

But God is.

"Blessed are they which do hunger and thirst after righteousness: for they shall be filled." (Matthew 5:6)

The men of Babel said, "We must build a tower and get through to God."

The Man of Bethlehem says, "Behold, I stand at the door, and knock: if any man . . . open the door, I will come in . . ." (Revelation 3:20)

To attain the peace that passes all understanding is not a question of activity, but a question of sensitivity. It is a question of recognition, not reorganization.

Look around you. He still comes to His own, and His own receive Him not. He is still in the world, and the world knows Him not. His light still shines in the darkness, and the darkness comprehends it not.

Let us examine God's approach to man and man's approach to God.

In the first place, man's efforts are infrequent and inconsistent. God's efforts are eternal.

Secondly, man tries to accomplish his ideals with material means. The men of Babel erected a gigantic structure of brick and mortar and stone.

They failed. They were worse off in the end than they were in the beginning, because confusion was all that they reached. They were farther away from God than they had been before.

Compare Jesse Gray and the fight for good housing with Governor Rockefeller's announcement of rebuilding Harlem:

> The proposed public authority would seek the construction in Harlem of an industrial park, office buildings, hotels, motels, a major shopping center, a city civic center, State offices, City-State education complex, and a Federal narcotics hospital. Its name will be HURDA—Harlem Urban Renewal Development Action.

Do you know what that means?

That means urban renewal equals Negro removal.

This has happened before. Under the wisest man of history, Solomon, they reached out for God. They built a permanent temple, rich in ornament, beauty, ritual. But the adventure ended in failure.

Man's approach to God fails whenever there is a material emphasis.

Too often when men are discouraged, disappointed, disillusioned, they have turned like the men of Babel to trying to find God in a building. There is an easier way, but there is no easy way.

Let him who would follow me take up his cross, deny himself, lay down his life for his brother, be slapped on both cheeks, walk the last mile, part his raiment with his friend, care not for his life, or what he shall eat or what he shall wear. Yea, all that shall live Godly shall suffer persecution.

Men never recaptured the sense of God until the centuries passed and one day God's man spoke:

> To what purpose is the multitude of your sacrifices unto me, saith the Lord . . . who hath required this at your hand . . . ?
> Wash ye, make you clean; put away the evil of your doings before mine eyes; cease to do evil;
> Learn to do well, seek judgment, relieve the oppressed, judge the fatherless, plead for the widow. (Isaiah 1:11–12, 16–17)

You cannot find God through brick and mortar.

> Why seek ye the living among the dead?
> He is not here, but is risen . . . (Luke 24:5–6)

You cannot attain a sense of God by what you do, but by what you are.

Too many are judging their lives by what they are doing,

by activities. But I come to ask the question "What are you?"

One thing the men of Babel were correct in—they knew that God was higher than they were. It was a partial attempt to try to find a vast truth.

But God is not above us in terms of distance, but only in terms of moral quality.

> For my thoughts are not your thoughts, neither are your ways my ways, saith the Lord.
> For as the heavens are higher than the earth, so are my ways higher than your ways, and my thoughts than your thoughts. (Isaiah 55:8–9)

Yes, God is beyond the reach of our lives. Yes, there is a definite chasm between us and God, but no building of brick and mortar can bridge that chasm. And this, now, is the fundamental point of our talk.

God comes to us down the valleys of life, and gives us the strength to climb to the mountain tops—not by our strength, not by our wisdom, but by His grace.

> . . . they that wait upon the Lord . . . shall mount up with wings as eagles; they shall run, and not be weary; and they shall walk, and not faint. (Isaiah 40:31)

What are you?
The answer: The Grace of God.

"Thy Will Be Done"

Not everyone that saith unto me, Lord, Lord, shall enter into the kingdom of heaven; but he that doeth the will of my Father which is in heaven.

MATTHEW 6:9–10

Our Father which art in heaven, Hallowed be thy name. Thy kingdom come. Thy will be done . . .

The crux of the problem of our world today is God versus man; beauty versus ugliness; peace versus war; contentment versus chaos; in substance, man's world versus God's world.

Wherever in this great worldly universe we find beauty and peace and all the things that go with them—security, happiness, love—we find that "Thy will is being done."

Wherever in this world we find ugliness, hatred and all the things that go with them—poverty, disease, crime, war—you can rest assured that not *Thy* will but *our* will is being done.

As we follow in His steps, as Christians, during this Lenten period, we need to come to a complete recognition that there can be no such thing as a family which rules out the concept of God.

This is why I call Abyssinian Baptist Church the family of God. Whenever man's will triumphs over God's will, there is discord, unhappiness and chaos.

It is absolutely impossible to be a part of man's material secular world and a part of the family of God. This is because the family of this world is temporary in all its aspects. Temporary in its relationships, in its home, in its security, and in the individual selves who comprise the unit.

This brings us to the inevitable conclusion that a true Christian, belonging to the family of God, looks beyond the temporary, affected by man's world, and grasps the complete significance of the permanent under the will of God.

A Christian family then is not a group which is broken up according to blood, race, nation or sex. The keynote is "Our Father."

In the family of God, it is not a question of husband, wife, father, mother, son or daughter who might be the controlling influence, but a question of God Almighty.

Because in any family that is controlled by any individual, however much love there may be, there can be nothing but a temporary relationship, temporary security and a temporary home.

A true family of God traces its genealogy back to the foot of the Cross, and follows it from there back to this day— two thousand years later—when close to a billion people profess the name of Jesus Christ as their brother.

The true family of God is one which recognizes that there is neither Jew nor Greek, bond nor free, male nor female—that all are one in Jesus.

The true family of God is one which recognizes as its sole bond that "as many as are led by the Spirit of God, they are the sons of God." (Romans 8:14) The true family is a family which is not our will, but "Thy will be done."

Therefore, as much as this may hurt you, I state emphatically that the family of this world must be secondary and the family of God must be primary.

In other words, we have a choice between citizenship in the Kingdom of God and citizenship in the kingdom of man.

> Our Father which art in heaven, Hallowed be thy name. Thy kingdom come. Thy will be done in earth, as it is in heaven. (Matthew 6:9–10)

This then must be our objective: that every one of us, young and old, must give unswerving allegiance to the establishment of the permanency of the family of God here and now in this world.

I stand this morning, Adam Clayton Powell, not as a Powell, not as a member of the Negro race, not even as an American—but as one who must do my utmost to see that the will of God is being done in *this* world.

I must first work toward putting the relationship of people on a permanent basis.

Second, toward bringing adequate security for all God's people—the war on poverty.

Third, toward making this world not only a neighborhood, but a brotherhood.

Fourth, to destroy every aspect of the temporary in our individual lives.

So, on this Communion morning, once again down through the centuries comes the voice of the Master crying to us who would follow: "Are ye able to drink of the cup that I shall drink of, and to be baptized with the baptism that I am baptized with?" (Matthew 20:22)

Let us respond to the Master: We are able to drink Thy cup and Thy will be done because we know: That each of us is a "child of the king" and he is our Savior.

Your Money and
Your Religion

HAGGAI 1:6–7

Ye have sown much, and bring in little; ye eat, but ye have not enough; ye drink, but ye are not filled with drink; ye clothe you, but there is none warm; and he that earneth wages earneth wages to put it into a bag with holes.

Thus saith the Lord of hosts; Consider your ways.

I have chosen as the background of this morning's talk the shortest book of the Old Testament. The book is scarcely more than one page—the book of Haggai.

The import of this book is all out of proportion to its size. It is a summary of four addresses delivered by the prophet Haggai between September 1 and December 31 in the year 520 B.C. The succession of Darius to the Persian throne in 521 was the occasion of insurrections all over his empire.

This "shaking of the nations" had stirred their hopes—politically as well as religiously. Haggai had the genius to seize this opportunity first. (Religious leaders must be as prominent in the political as in the church.)

The experiences of the last seventy years, beginning with the Exile and continuing with the disillusioning consequences on their return, had gravely shattered the political hopes of the people.

Haggai came upon the scene with one purpose—to concentrate the hopes and efforts of his people in organizing their religious community and therefore building a temple to God.

Scarcely anything is known of his personal life. He appeared upon the scene suddenly and disappeared just as suddenly. On the basis of the second chapter you may suppose that he was born in Judah before the catastrophe of 586 B.C.

Therefore, he was one of a small company among the exiles who had seen the former temple in all of its glory. If so, he must have been a very old man when he prophesied, which may have accounted for the brevity of his public activities.

The exhortation to build the temple, from which we draw the background for our thoughts, was addressed to the civil governor, Zerubbabel, and to the religious head of the community, Joshua.

The people had been disheartened by the bad harvest: "they had sown much and brought in little." A drought had been upon the land, withering away everything that they had planted. The brilliant promises of Isaiah had not been fulfilled.

They were disillusioned people.

Prices were high; wages low. It seemed as if the money just dropped through holes in their pockets.

Sincerely they argued that the time had not yet come to build the temple. Their resources were too pitifully inadequate.

Their sad plight showed plainly, but God was still angry with them. It was unreasonable for them to emulate David in his enthusiasm to build Jehovah a house.

But Haggai met this news (as prophets always must) by putting a moral interpretation on the people's disaster. He said: Consider your ways. You have neglected God's house but you live in houses covered with costly woodwork. You walked around looking for much and it came to little.

Today it seems that our wages are put into a bag with holes.

Extravagance is such a bag: spending more than your income justifies; living so near to your income it is impossible not to go beyond it. A good way to meet this problem is to either earn more or spend less.

Waste: Some people think waste is extravagance. Waste may be of a thing that is necessary—food, fuel, money, land, produce, talent.

Excess: This is like extravagance and waste but it is extravagance and waste employed on yourself and to the detriment of yourself. It means spending any large proportion of what you have on things which minister chiefly to pride and glory—to say nothing of the evil side of one's life.

What should I do? "Labour not to be rich . . ." (Proverbs 23:4)

First, it is impossible for most people to become rich.

Second, the cost of laboring to be rich is exorbitant: in energy—a fierce battle. In time—a long battle, weary toil, uncertainty.

A wealth-seeker is liable to sink into low materialism.

Third, the attainment of riches is often disappointing. It brings new cares, anxieties, fears, and of what value are they to your heart and your mind?

Fourth, laboring to be rich leads to a neglect of the nobler things of life: the culture of one's mind; social intercourse; the service of God.

But we have inherited this one fact: we must put God first in all things—this means God's house, God's program, God's people and God's inner self in your life.

> Jesus answered and said unto him, If a man love me, he will keep my words: and my Father will love him, and we will come unto him, and make our abode with him.
>
> He that loveth me not keepeth not my sayings: and the word which ye hear is not mine, but the Father's which sent me.
>
> These things have I spoken unto you, being yet present with you.
>
> But the Comforter, which is the Holy Ghost, whom the Father will send in my name, he shall teach you all things, and bring all things to your remembrance, whatsoever I have said unto you.
>
> Peace I leave with you, my peace I give unto you: not as the world giveth, give I unto you. Let not your heart be troubled, neither let it be afraid.
>
> Ye have heard how I said unto you, I go away, and come again unto you. If ye loved me, ye would rejoice, because

I said, I go unto the Father: for my Father is greater than I.

And now I have told you before it come to pass, that, when it is come to pass, ye might believe.

Hereafter I will not talk much with you: for the prince of this world cometh, and hath nothing in me.

But that the world may know that I love the Father; and as the Father gave me commandment, even so I do. Arise, let us go hence. (John 14:23–31)

Jesus was closer to being penniless than any man you or I have ever known.

Yet, he left the greatest will ever made. No notary witnessed it; no seal legalized it; no one signed it.

It was committed only to the men who loved Him, and decades were to pass before they wrote it down.

He left the secret of peace. How much is peace worth—to a home rent by discord; to a mind that's out of tune with its world; to a nation at war?

He left a promise of power. Our world is power mad but not mad for the right kind of power.

Jesus left the promise of power to bear, believe, hope, endure, forgive, forget, trust, and to lay down one's life for a friend or place it in God's hands without any fear.

He left a command: "That ye love one another; as I have loved you . . ." (John 13:34)

He left a comforter: "And I will pray the Father, and he shall give you another Comforter, that he may abide with you for ever . . ." (John 14:16)

The Search for Freedom

ACTS 22:27–28

Then the chief captain came, and said unto him, Tell me, art thou a Roman? He said, Yea.

And the chief captain answered, With a great sum obtained I this freedom. And Paul said, But I was free born.

GALATIANS 5:1

Stand fast therefore in the liberty wherewith Christ hath made us free, and be not entangled again with the yoke of bondage.

Let us discuss as briefly as possible the development of the concept of freedom. The first written statement on freedom we know is God speaking to Moses on Mount Sinai in the twenty-fifth chapter of Leviticus, saying, ". . . proclaim liberty throughout all the land unto all the inhabitants thereof: it shall be a jubilee unto you."

In the ninth century before Jesus, Lycurgus in Greece gave to the citizens a constitution which made the country united, strong and subject to the most stable government the world has ever seen. This was the first constitution in the world.

In the sixth century, Solon was commissioned to rewrite the laws, and brought new freedom and new responsibility. The spirit of humanity prevailed in the life of the ancient Greeks.

This Athenian concept of liberty endured for centuries.

The concept of liberty exercised by these ancients is what today would be called political liberty—the right to participate in the determination of government, the right to choose leaders —but with no safeguards of individual liberties.

Aristotle declared that the ideal state would be a state of democratic absolutism. Cicero, just about fifty years before Jesus, clearly indicated that any law passed contrary to the law of nature was void, thus for the first time setting up a standard of legislation.

Tacitus, some fifty years after Jesus, stated: "In peace, representative government; in war, generals; in peril, dictators."

For one thousand two hundred years, the world slumbered in a morass of oppression, but on June 15, 1215, King John of England signed the Magna Carta, which is regarded as the basis of the constitutions of the English-speaking world.

This said that no man's body shall be taken, imprisoned, outlawed, banished, damaged in any way except by the judgment of his peers.

In 1628, the House of Lords and the House of Commons passed the Petition of Right, which said that people may not be sacrificed to the interest, policy and ambition of those who wield political power.

John Locke, the British philosopher, in 1690 published the first statement that government is not an absolute power, but a conditional moral trust. People have the right and the duty to throw it out if it fails or violates the trust imposed upon it.

In 1762, Rousseau, the French philosopher, declared that government exists only at the pleasure of the governed and with their consent to its actions. He coined the great phrase: "Liberty, equality, fraternity."

In 1774, the First Continental Congress convened in America, and it was declared that everyone was entitled to life, liberty and property.

And on July 4, 1776, a committee including Thomas Jefferson, John Adams, Benjamin Franklin, Roger Sherman and Philip Livingston drew up the Declaration of Independence, which states: "We hold these truths to be self-evident, that all men are created equal."

When the Constitution of the United States was presented to the states for ratification, the people were so fearful lest individual liberties were not protected that they pronounced the Constitution "dangerous" to the liberties of the states and citizens and they demanded as a condition to ratification a statement for limitation of federal action.

The resultant first ten amendments are called the Bill of Rights, of which Article I guarantees the four freedoms:

1. Freedom of *religion.*
2. Freedom of *speech.*
3. Freedom of the *press.*
4. Freedom of *assembly.*

One hundred fifty years later, Franklin Delano Roosevelt translated the four freedoms into the objectives of World War II:

1. Freedom of religion.
2. Freedom of speech.
3. Freedom from want.
4. Freedom from fear.

POLITICAL FREEDOM VS. SPIRITUAL FREEDOM

Man's search for ultimate truths has been a relentless search for freedom in terms of political liberty and individual liberty. But the reason the practices of freedom have not changed appreciably from the days of the Athenians is that no one can be free until he has been freed from slavery of self.

This inner freedom comes only from the power of God. No man can free his inner self without the help of God and the teachings of Jesus. "And ye shall know the truth, and the truth shall make you free." (John 8:32)

Unless we accept this, we are in chains.

Our problem therefore is: political freedoms may wax and wane and individual liberties may expand or contract, but none of these fluctuating conditions must be permitted to change our pursuit of freedom for our inner selves.

> Stand fast therefore in the liberty wherewith Christ hath made us free, and be not entangled again with the yoke of bondage. (Galatians 5:1)

Therefore the victory in the whole fight for freedom rests in one's intimate acquaintanceship with Jesus Christ. "If the Son therefore shall make you free, ye shall be free indeed." (John 8:36)

Only you can break your yoke.

Only black people can lead the black revolution and black people into their promised land.

The Techniques of Triumph

ROMANS 12:21

Be not overcome of evil, but overcome evil with good.

Unless you believe with me that the church is still in the process of growing, then this sermon is of no value. But history supports me through several divine manifestations:

The sainted men of the Old Testament, groping in the dark, trying to find the Messiah.

The coming of the Messiah.

The work of the first generation of disciples.

Christian thinking under the Roman Empire.

The triumph of Christianity over paganism in 326 A.D.

The Dark Ages of the Church.

The Age of Papacy.

The saints of the Middle Ages—Abelard and Thomas Aquinas.

The Protestant Reformation, and today the Ecumenical Movement.

There are in the church today two groups of people—the religious rationalizers and the religiously inquisitive.

Religious rationalizers are devout, honest. Religion is something they acquired in their childhood. It is precious; it is holy; it is complete; it is finished. There's nothing more to learn about it; you just sit back and enjoy it and use it. Their religion is taken for granted. This leads to complacency and deterioration.

The religiously inquisitive are the movers in the church.

In order for the church to grow, I call this morning for sincere radical, intellectual reconstruction of our religion on a continuing basis.

Even the mind of God is ever on the move and Jeremiah foresaw it when he said: "Behold, the days come, saith the Lord, that I will make a new covenant with the house of Israel . . ." (Jeremiah 31:31)

Religion is growth, not stagnation. The thinking Christians are the religiously inquisitive.

The need is for daring. As the tensions of these days continue to thrust themselves upon our consciousness, again we come face to face with two views: (1) those who would escape; and (2) those who would overcome.

The escapists turn to books, movies, theater, gambling, dissipation. No problem can ever be solved by escape.

To overcome is what I call for now—men and women who would dare to overcome. This is the heart of the Black Revolution. "Deep in my heart, I do believe, we will overcome someday."

Remember, religion is a power which develops the hero in the man at the expense of the coward.

The real danger of religion is believing too much and being too little.

True growing religion does not adhere to any particular dogma or loyalty or church standard.

True religion is a daring faith, faith in the reality of the things that are unseen and eternal; a devotion of life to these unseen things.

What then are the ways of overcoming—the techniques of triumph?

1. *Point of view to be taken:* "A thousand years are but as yesterday or as the watch in the night. Why should I limit my vision to this petty period of twenty or thirty years? I lift up my

eyes to the hills, hills that stand unshaken amid the tempest, always among the stars."

2. *Line of action to be followed:* Have a sense of direction to move, and move nonviolently. This is a classless, raceless philosophy.

3. *Lesson of experience to be learned:* "We have trouble on every side, yet are not distressed. We are perplexed, but not in despair, persecuted but not forsaken, cast down but not destroyed, always bearing about us the dying of the Lord Jesus that the life of Jesus might be made manifest in us."

4. *Vision of faith to behold:* Down through the purple centuries, there have marched two faiths, which have ever guarded and controlled the lives of men. One, faith in the material, and the other, faith in the spiritual.

Oh, yes, there is an outer world of force, of things—no doubt about that. But it is a changing world, an undependable world. Far greater is the inner world of the spirit—the imponderables which cannot be weighed; the intangibles which cannot be touched; the inaudible which cannot be heard.

No more can we feel sunshine without looking at the sun; or the wind blowing without seeing it; or the sea turbulence without knowing its cause.

Conquerors have come and gone.

Empires have risen and fallen.

The greatest have ruled but for a few years, and the mightiest empires, but for a few centuries.

Why should we think that the powers of today are more powerful than those of Alexander, Caesar or Napoleon?

David said: "Fret not thyself because of evildoers . . . For they shall soon be cut down like the grass . . . Trust in the Lord, and do good . . ." (Psalms 37:1–3)

I call therefore for daring men and women—men and women who have character, conviction; who know the eternal distinction between right and wrong; who will listen to the spirit rather than the law; who will possess a joy that is unspeakable in a world of sorrow; who in their hour of duress and travail lean upon their God.

Is this a dream? No. Roll back the clouds of the past. Push back the horizon and bring in the omnipotent, the omniscient, the omnipresent God.

Facing the Future

Now faith is the substance of things hoped for, the evidence of things not seen.

Let your light so shine before men, that they may see your good works, and glorify your Father which is in heaven.

As we bring our 155th Anniversary to a close in 1963, and face the future, it is my humble conviction that the major crisis facing all of us today—as individuals and as the collective body of the church—is the problem of making up our minds. Too many of us are drifting. And even those who are not, resent new ideas, innovations, and prefer the debilitating security of the status quo.

This was the lesson that Joshua tried to give his people. He told them what God had already done; how He had led Abraham, Isaac and Jacob. When they were in trouble, He sent Moses and Aaron to liberate them. When enemies came against them, He destroyed them. He even brought them to a land for which they did not labor, to live in cities which they did not build, to eat of vineyards which they did not plant.

Then the old man, Joshua, says to them, On the basis of all this, you should put away any other gods. But, whether you do or not, make up your minds.

Don't make up your mind tomorrow or next year, but on this day choose whom you will serve.

At the turn of the century, the sixteenth minister of the Abyssinian Baptist Church, the Rev. Dr. Charles Satchel Morris, led the Abyssinian Baptist Church from Waverly Place to Fortieth Street. Fifty-five years ago this month—November, 1908—my father came to this church at the occasion of its centennial. And, a dozen years later, he began to lead the people of

Abyssinian from Fortieth Street to this spot, West 138th Street.

A little over two years ago, under my ministry, we led the church from out of these walls into the new buildings surrounding us.

We have made marvelous progress. Our expansion program has undergone a period of stress and tribulations. Many of us, including your minister, have made great sacrifices, almost beyond our capacities to bear. What I am appealing for now, as we face the future, is to continue our sacrificing. But more than that, I am appealing to those of you who live around the body of the church to get into the heart of it.

> . . . the Lord thy God shall bless thee in the land whither thou goest to possess it.
> But if thine heart turn away . . .
> I denounce unto you this day, that ye shall surely perish . . . (Deuteronomy 30:16–18)

The besetting sin of all peoples, and especially Christians, is the corruption of complacency. We could have stayed in Waverly Place and remained just another church. We could have rested on Fortieth Street and been just another church. We could have stayed complacently within these walls and been just another religious mediocrity. There is no particular magic in the name Abyssinian Baptist or Adam Clayton Powell.

The magic is the name of God.

Where God is, there is life, action, vitality, progress. The greatest critique of our modern complacency was made by Amos when he said, "Woe unto them that are at ease in Zion . . ." (6:1)

Let us take the example of Moses. He refused to be complacent as the son of Pharaoh's daughter. But he did not make his choice on the basis of the temporary or the temporal.

First, he chose to suffer affliction with God's people rather than enjoy the pleasures of sin for a season.

Second, he esteemed the reproach of God greater than all the riches and treasures of Egypt.

As we face the future, be assured of one thing: That with or without you, God's kingdom marches on. That with or without you, the Church of God is built upon a rock and all the forces of complacency, compromise and conservatism shall not prevail against it.

As you face the future as an individual, face it with action.

For it is upon the basis of our works that we are evaluated by man and by God.

> I know thy works . . . [and] because thou art lukewarm . . .
> I will spew thee out of my mouth. . . .
> Behold, I stand at the door, and knock: if any man hear my voice, and open the door, I will come in to him . . . to him that overcometh will I grant to sit with me in my throne . . . (Revelation 3:15–16, 20–21)

Who sits with God today?

The people who face the future with Him.

Abel, who offered a more excellent sacrifice than Cain.

Enoch, who walked with God.

Noah, who faced the future on God's advice and prepared an ark.

Abraham, who faced the future blindly, not knowing whither he went. And, when he was tried, even offered up his own son, Isaac.

Isaac, who blessed Jacob and Esau, because he wanted them to face the future—"concerning things to come." (Hebrews 11:20)

Jacob, who, even when he was dying, blessed both the sons of Joseph.

These are the ones who sit with God.

And many others—Gideon, Barak, Samson, David, Samuel—because they didn't stand still.

They subdued kingdoms, wrought righteousness, obtained promises, stopped the mouths of lions, quenched the violence of fire, escaped the edge of the sword, out of weakness were made strong, waxed valiant in fight, turned to flight the armies of the Aeolians.

In the face of cruel mockings and scourgings of bonds and imprisonments, they were stoned, they were sawn asunder, tempted, slain; they wandered about, destitute, afflicted, tormented, but kept their hand in God's hand and received not just a promise, but God provided some better things.

And what about Jesus?

He endured the Cross, despised the shame, but faced the future of eternal life because he believed in the Redemption of the Holy Spirit.

> Wherefore, seeing we also are compassed about with so great a cloud of witnesses, let us lay aside every weight, and the sin which doth so easily beset us, let us run with patience the race that is set before us . . . (Hebrews 12:1)

Do You Really Believe in God?

JANUARY 23, 1955

II CHRONICLES 20:20

. . . Believe in the Lord your God, so shall ye be established; believe his prophets, so shall ye prosper.

The gloomy dean, Dr. Inge, of the University of Chicago, has just suggested that he views with suspicion the large number of people who are attending church and who are joining church. He does not know whether they are really believing in God or whether religion has become a fad.

Dr. Morton White, philosopher of Harvard University, has just stated that most people who are turning to religion are not necessarily turning to God. People are religious today because they feel it is good to be religious—not because they are convinced of being religious by the existence of God.

This leads me to ask, What is religion?

Is it a species of poetry? Is it a variety of shared experience? Is it ethical culture? Is it insight into a man's nature?

These are popular concepts of modern intellectuals, but you will note there is no voice identifying religion with God.

What we are trying to do with religion is make it fill the void created by the dissolving effects of science. This is the end of a hot war between science and religion and may be the beginning of a cold war within the field of religion.

In the eighteenth and nineteenth centuries, plans began to drive away the mystery and the reason in faith. Logic and faith were thought of as incompatible; therefore religion fell back on emotions.

Emotional arguments for God came into vogue. The world was swept with religious revival, so much so that John

285

Wesley said, "The human heart is being strangely warmed."

Science, the nineteenth century's bringer of light, has become the twentieth century's caster of darkness. Somewhere in our modern world between the mysteries of the atom and the endless wastes of space, man seems to drift in helpless ignorance of the powers and purposes that hold him.

The universe, which once seemed to be clockwork, now throbs with awesome power before which modern men, including scientists, are now turning to God. Man's emotions no longer lead him, easily, to God.

No less than 96 percent of the United States' citizens believe in God, according to a survey made by George Gallup.

What do people consider the most convincing argument for God's existence?

1. The order and majesty of the world around them.
2. There must be a creator to explain the origin of man and the world.
3. There is proof of God in the Bible or the church authority.
4. Past experiences in life make us think there is a God.
5. Believing in God gives much comfort.

In favoring the argument based on order in the universe, Americans are charting a new swing of an old pendulum. Medieval man also saw God in the order of things, but his universe fitted snugly around him with the world at the center.

St. Thomas Aquinas formulated his five proofs of God's existence with a respect for logic. He rated the proofs derived from the order and majesty of the world. These were his proofs:

1. The passing from power to the act or motion implies an unmoved power.
2. Similarly, there must be an uncaused first cause that possesses in itself the reason for its existence.
3. The existence of being whose nonexistence is possible implies the existence of a necessary need.

4. The scale of perfection evidenced in our universe implies the existence of an absolutely perfect being.

5. The order and majesty of the world around them.

The fact that the argument about God giving comfort shows up in the Gallup poll suggests that religion has gone soft, but since this proof ranks last there is some mitigation of the churchmen's fears.

There are two significant omissions in the Gallup polls:

1. The argument by the testimony of moral conscience, which leads men to God through consideration of the presence of truth in the human mind.

2. The proof by universal consensus, which holds that if there is no God, how is it possible that practically all people, everywhere, spontaneously reach the conclusion that there is a God?

The question should no longer be: Shall I be religious? Shall I be a Jew? Shall I be a Catholic? Shall I be a Protestant?

The question to be asked first is: Do I believe in God?

Because, for me, in my Bible, there is no religion without God!

Let the scholars in our schools of higher religious instruction argue about the religion of God.

But let the masses say: I believe in God; He is my Savior!

The Negro and
His Church

PSALMS 68:31

Princes shall come out of Egypt; Ethiopia shall soon stretch out her hands unto God.

MATTHEW 28:19

Go ye therefore, and teach all nations, baptizing them in the name of the Father, and of the Son, and of the Holy Ghost.

As we stand upon the threshold of this new year, and as the fight for civil rights legislation begins in Congress, I would like to address myself to the Negro and his church.

When the average Negro is asked who his enemies are, he will immediately reply, "Wallace, Maddox, Eastland and Thurmond." This, of course, is true, but I say this morning that we have some enemies within our race and forces working against our progress that we seemingly are not conscious of. I can think of five.

1. *Divisions among ourselves.* There is no unity, no in-gathering, no sense of racial pride that enables us to pull together to solve our own problems. We must stop blaming everything on the white man.

2. *Misleadership.* We only have "Negro leaders." Whites have financiers, corporation presidents, Presidents, governors and educators. We have "Negro leaders."

3. *Indifference toward our own problems.* Negroes think that things are so much better than they used to be that we are all right. We're like that weary old black man who plodded the back roads of Mississippi with his head down, singing, "Been down so long, down looks up to me."

4. *Refusal to use civil rights and divine rights which we already possess.* Boycotts and ballots, if we used them intelligently, could bring us more power.

5. *An endless and vain search for a substitute for the Negroes' church in politics, education, economics and social life.*

The Negroes' church itself should be the political, educational, economic and social capital of the Negro race.

Here stands the Negroes' church. All it needs is a regenerated rank-and-file following, motivated by the desire to elevate the masses, activated by a passion for right, and surcharged with unquenchable zeal.

Then, and only then, shall be brought to pass the thing that was written: "Princes shall come out of Egypt. Ethiopia shall soon stretch out her hands unto God."

This is the crying need of the hour for our people, for us, ourselves, to restore to the individual his supreme worth as a human being.

It can only be accomplished through the Negroes' church.

In this hour of chaos and crisis, in this hour when the black man's destiny is being shaped for the next hundred years, we must have:

First, a mass base for the Negro church involving all of the black masses, not just a middle-class select few.

Second, radically sincere leadership, which will respect no one but God and the black masses, who cry out like Peter of old, "We must obey God, rather than man."

Third, a militancy based upon the power of nonviolence, which neither compromises nor knows a middle ground.

Fourth, an implicit faith that the new day is here, for one day it shall come: one day the lion and the lamb shall lie down together.

One day the trees of the forest shall clap their hands together for joy.

One day the skies shall be split, and one day the cry shall go up: "Victory!"

Therefore, in the blackest hour, I do not despair.

I, Adam Powell, a member of a minority that is poor, despised and oppressed, will look beyond this gathering gloom, and catch the morning rays of the rising sun of a new world.

It may not come in my lifetime, but one day a new world shall come.

Yes, upon the surface, many times down through the centuries, the cause of progress seemed to have been lost.

The water was troubled by those who wanted to rule the world for themselves.

But, ever and anon, beneath the surface, the Eternal One has moved the great tides of life with unfailing accuracy and minute precision.

The oppression we face as Negroes today is not the first, the worst, or the last crisis. But I assure you that always, in the darkest hour, there appeared a man and a mass guided by God.

> For ye see your calling, brethren, how that not many wise men after the flesh, not many mighty, not many noble, are called:
>
> But God hath chosen the foolish things of the world to confound the wise; and God hath chosen the weak things of the world to confound the things which are mighty;
>
> And base things of the world, and things which are despised, hath God chosen, yea, and things which are not, to bring to nought things that are . . . (I Corinthians 1:26–28)